Remarkably Intact

Angels Are No Strangers to Chains

Remarkably Intact

Angels Are No Strangers to Chains

Celia Belt

with Alison Raffalovich

Broer Books

First Edition

ISBN: 978-1-7321040-0-6

Dedication

This book is dedicated to my children, Justin, Jarred, and Hillary,
my grandson, Korben, and my late husband, Randy.
It is the love I received from each of you that carried me
through this writing process.

Giving Back

A portion of proceeds from the sale of *Remarkably Intact*
will benefit burn survivors, their families, and those
who have lost a loved one to a burn injury.

Table of Contents

Prologue

I am emotionally and physically exhausted as I pull up the tree-lined drive at my quaint ranch in Bandera, Texas. My day had begun in the early dawn hours when my phone—which is at my side twenty-four hours a day, every day—rang. A burn survivor was being admitted to the unit at Brooke Army Medical Center. After many years of volunteering there, I knew my role well. Little sleep would come to me that night, as it would for the new patient and his family. I know this because, I, too, am a burn survivor.

The burn patient was an Army GI who'd been badly injured when his vehicle hit an incendiary device in Iraq. He was initially stabilized at an army hospital in Europe and was sent to San Antonio for his long path to recovery—if he had one.

Hours passed in a blur as I helped him get settled and worked with his family. I arranged for their housing nearby and got them acclimated with the treatment center routine. I could see in their eyes that they were trying to adjust to the shock. The family's strong father, husband, loved one was in excruciating pain. We talked for a long time, and I listened as they voiced their shock, fear, and sadness. I tried to gently prepare them for the seemingly endless round of surgeries, physical therapy, and emotional trauma that lay ahead, drawing on my own experience as a burn survivor and that of the thousands my organization has assisted through the years.

It was early evening by the time I left them. I assured the family I'd be back the next day—and the day after that—for as long as they needed a loving, guiding hand.

When I reach home, I step onto the back porch and breathe fresh hill-country air and take in the breathtaking views of the hills that surround our property. It's tough to describe, the hills are miles away, yet I feel that with my outstretched arm I can touch each one and they become a part of me. I feel a power and a strength from them that can only be described as otherworldly. Afterward, I feed my three dogs—imported German shepherds Kurtz and Taboo, and Kenji, the toy American Eskimo. My crazy Mekong bobtail cat Bobo, who thinks he's a dog, curls up beside me on the chair. I down some fruit, sip tea, then head to the barn to care for my sweet little Sicilian miniature donkey, Lilly, and my Friesian horses, Broer and Toranado. As with all nights like this, I wait for a phone call from my husband, Randy. His work takes him around the world and living apart means that every phone call is a precious gift.

The rolling hills of Texas, it's where I find peace. I have the unconditional love of my husband and from the animals that fill my life. They're nourishment for the soul and give me strength to get up each day, providing support as I work with my beloved patients on their healing journeys. There's a certain harmony to my life, the yin and yang seem to be in perfect balance and I feel blessed each and every day to be a part of this glorious world of mine. I await the sunset and the magnificent peace it brings me each night. The colors speak to me in words of love.

Tired as I am, there is always work to do, and I want to fit in a few more hours before the sweet embrace of sleep. I need to finalize another grant application. Our foundation tirelessly seeks the support of donors and partners to meet our patient-base needs. I have an upcoming engagement and want to finalize the speech. My life may seem like chaos to some, but I find a great deal of satisfaction in the work I do.

To build awareness of our mission and connect with as many burn survivors as possible, I accept speaking engagements—everything from small support groups to a capacity crowd at the Pentagon. Not long ago, I gratefully accepted the Fisher House/Newman's Own Award on behalf of the Moonlight Fund as the top nonprofit in the nation improving the quality of life of wounded military members and their families. Receiving that award was humbling and I was happy to have Randy by my side. We had dinner the first night at Admiral Winnefeld's home, who at that time was the Vice Chairman of the Joint Chiefs of Staff. He and his wife, Mary, were incredibly gracious. Incidentally, their home once belonged to General Patton. It is filled with history, mementos, and many photos that are now part of the home's archives.

The award ceremony was the next day and we were off to the Pentagon. There we spent time with the Chairman of the Joint Chiefs of Staff, General Martin Dempsey, his wife, Deanie, and assorted other guests. It was an amazing experience to speak in that hallowed room with General Dempsey seated to my left. Everyone present—military, socialites, and a healthy number of celebrities—was there to honor the work of the Moonlight Fund. As I began my speech, I searched for Randy; my husband was seated in the first row. His relaxed expression instilled all the confidence I needed.

—◆—

A few days after the solider was admitted, my phone rings. It's Annie, a young mother in Ohio who, after several reconstructive surgeries, was recently discharged from the hospital. Unfortunately, she can't afford the much-needed physical therapy. I located and hired a physical therapist for her who had worked with other burn survivors, and Annie calls to tell me she's had her first session. She said it was painful hard work. But

Annie is determined to stay the course until she recovers sufficient range of motion, regaining the ability to cook and care for her children. I assure her that we will find a way to cover additional physical therapy sessions for as long as she needs them. This call is like so many others. The needs of burn survivors are great, and to this day there remains very little support.

Despite long hours of walking through the painful and tragic effects of burns and their ongoing struggles, I am grateful for my life and an opportunity to help this underserved community of survivors. I am fulfilled by my mission. Founded in 1998, the Moonlight Fund has touched the lives of 10,000 burn survivors and their families and we're not slowing down. It's a bare-bones operation that includes me, my wonderful daughter Hillary, an outside accountant, a pro-bono social media director, thirty-seven incredible volunteers, and a very accomplished, well-connected board of directors. With this structure of low overhead and expert guidance, we accomplish amazing things and dedicate as many resources as possible to helping our patients continue on their healing journeys. The funds we raise and the resources of our partners go directly to where they're needed most. We're also committed to transparency, which earned us a Platinum rating from GuideStar.

If that introduction was the whole story, I could write an interesting book about my twenty years of building Moonlight Fund and walking alongside the suffering of burn survivors. But there's more. Much more. It's been a long and sometimes very dark journey to where I am—and who I am—today. It's hard to believe that I have only an eighth-grade education but went on to become an executive in food manufacturing and real estate sales. I'm a survivor of childhood abuse, yet I've had the great good fortune to raise three wonderful children in a loving and safe environment. I'm a burn survivor who's dedicated years to ensuring that fellow burn survivors are not alone. That they get the emotional, medical, and financial services they need to build a new life. I was a bullied, ostracized schoolgirl who is now in demand as a public speaker at venues ranging from small support groups to the Pentagon, from roundtables to radio broadcasts and television interviews. I married the love of my life, a gift many people never experience.

When I was a child, I never imagined that, one day, each and every one of my dreams would come true. It's been a decades-long, tortuous path that included exquisitely tender moments, alternating with pain, struggle, and tough decisions—some of which I would come to regret, some of which I know kept me strong. I did all this in hopes of moving toward the fulfilling life I feared I couldn't have and didn't deserve. I am blessed each and every day by the love and friendship of many people I've met through this singular mission.

I'm sharing my story in hopes that it provides inspiration to anyone who is struggling with their own difficult path, whether you are a burn survivor, abuse survivor, or someone who's been thrown a tough curveball in life. My way forward was not the most direct path, and I am not proud of some of my choices and decisions. Yet, today I have peace and beauty. I am comfortable in my own burned skin that I don't cover or hide. I live with my entire terrible history, out in the open for others to see. After decades of trying to be the person who I thought others wanted me to be, of trying to hide secrets in my past that I thought would make others reject or pity me, I now choose honesty and directness. I hope that in some small way my story can give you the courage to find your own way forward, and to find your own place of peace and acceptance. I also hope that you'll accept my raunchy and insane sense of humor, because it is with laughter and sarcasm—which I developed and honed as survival tools—that I find fun in the worst of times and that many times humor is the only way to survive.

Speaking at the Pentagon, accepting the award from General Martin Dempsey for the Moonlight Fund, after being chosen as the top non profit in the U.S.

Montel Williams offers his congratulations at the Pentagon

Randy and me with Admiral James Winnefeld at his home in Washington D.C.

Oh my Broer, my gentle giant

Home and safe, my two favorite words

My German Shepard, Kurtz, and Friesians, Toranado and Broer

My German Shepard, Taboo, and me during a photo shoot for Randy

With Ember, the wolf

CHAPTER ONE

Broken

Didn't you hear me say "ouch?" You left too many bruises this time, you will surely be found out

One day, any day, all I can do is hope, cry and pray

Why? Why do I cry...because I said "ouch"

I said it and begged it, I fed it and loathed it

I meant it to be just as I said it

When you are found out, it will be the day my angels take their revenge

Yes, they will rescue me, I know they will, until they do—I'll just sit here on the porch, begging for them to come

I've had my fill

Yes, I've had my fill of nightmares and little white lies that nearly become reality in my young mind

I'm quiet as a mouse, even when the "ouch" is more than I can bear

I know you'll be found out, I know you will

You see, my Angels are coming, they will hold me tight in this deep dark fright

And when they do, you'll no longer be able to hurt me

They'll throw you to the darkness, where you will know the pain of the fire and I hope that's where you'll stay.

Until then, I'll just say "ouch"

For as long as I can remember, I'd always been told I was broken. It all began when I was 21 months with a large pot of boiling water containing my infant brother's baby bottles. I could hear him crying and I wanted to help. I raised my arms, reaching for the pot—that's when it happened. Hearing my screams, my mother rushed to my side, swiftly removing my shirt. To her horror, my tender skin came off with it.

As a parent now, I find it painful to imagine how my mother felt in those moments. This must have been one of the truest sufferings of a parent's heart. I was rushed to the hospital with burns to my face, arm, torso, and thighs. During my hospital stay, things became worse and I developed pseudomonas and pneumonia. As my condition deteriorated, the doctors told my parents they should prepare for the worst and summon their priest. We had only recently moved to Rockford, and my parents had not yet established a relationship with the local church. They went to the closest Catholic parish and explained that their child needed to be given last rites. Would he be so kind as to do so? Surprisingly, the priest refused. They were not members of his church, and there was nothing he could do. After that, my entire family left the Catholic faith and became Lutherans. I've often joked that I lived to spite the Catholic church. All in all, it would be months before I was out of the woods, but I made it through and I continued to survive.

Once I was well enough to withstand the procedures, the grafting process began, using tissue from my buttocks. My parents were determined to seek out a way to "fix" me. I realize now, it was more than the scars they were attempting to remove—it was the truth. The revolving door of doctors, clinics, and painful procedures offered no closure or cure and only confirmed in my mind that I was "broken."

Unfortunately, I had a reaction that caused my body to send excess collagen to the area of my burns and to where the donor tissue was harvested. This resulted in very painful, ropy hypertrophic scarring.

In turn, this development resulted in even more surgeries, attempts to control or remove the dense scar tissue. I can still hear the desperation in my plastic surgeon's voice as he told my mother that I would need to go to Shriners Hospital for children who had suffered burns. He'd cared for me so lovingly, for so many years, and to this day he holds a special place in my heart. Yet, becoming a Shriners' patient was a huge stepping stone to my emotional recovery. During each visit, as we sat in the waiting room, I was surrounded by children who'd suffered burn injuries much worse than mine. There was a pivotal shift in my mind and for the first time in my life, I felt empathy.

My childhood became a painful, endless cycle of surgeries, casts, and pain. I underwent thirty-one surgeries before age nine, and would subject myself to countless more until I was thirty-one. Well into my adult life, I found myself seeking out one doctor after another in an effort to remove my scars. I was obsessed with the notion that I could change my life by removing that part of myself. By doing so, I would become the woman of my dreams. But the horrible truth is that many of the procedures caused additional scarring and led to more surgeries. There came a point where I gave up and gave into the notion that short sleeves and bathing suits, would simply never be a part of my life.

I recall one period in particular. It was right before fourth grade. I decided that drastic changes to my appearance and persona would alter my entire circumstance. Until this time, I went by my middle name, LaVon. I was named after my mother, Celia, and my favorite aunt, Rhonda LaVon. I had never been called Celia; I assumed it was easier for my family to have just one Celia in the house. It wasn't a bad gig, going by LaVon, the name of my bright and beautiful aunt. But I had to flee my past to create a new future. That year I started school with a new name—Celia. I cut off all my hair and reinvented my wardrobe. I was sure that the new name, hair, and clothing would disguise me. I was positive the children at school would not recognize me. My cleverly laid plan did not work, and I was heartbroken on the first day of school when classmates simply continued to call me LaVon.

But this is only a small piece of my whole story. It wasn't until years later that I discovered the true circumstances behind my scalding. My father was an abusive problem drinker. He'd lost his temper because I wanted to fetch my brother's bottle. I hadn't reached for the pot, as I believed. He'd thrown the boiling water over me.

This was the reason my parents wanted no visible reminder of the horrible scars—which were, ironically, in many ways made worse by some of the treatments. It was our "secret," and one that was never to be discussed with anyone. Along with my burns, at an early age, I learned the craft of secret keeping, spinning lies, and being someone else. My parents stood solidly by their public persona. My mother, the tall, striking beauty queen, and my father, equally attractive, flying his private plane and enjoying a solid career.

It wasn't just the rounds of futile treatments that cemented my sense of brokenness. Each morning, I stood still as my mother applied heavy makeup to cover my scars. She also carefully chose clothing that had the best chance of covering up my scars. Every time a camera appeared for a family or school photograph, they showed me how to pose "just so." Eventually, things like photograph taking became an instinctive, practiced physical maneuver. I would quickly angle myself so that my "good side" showed and position my body so the camera lens didn't highlight my scars. I learned to smile the bright smile of a happy child who was living a "normal" life.

Even today, I catch myself standing in positions so the scars are less noticeable. Despite this, I discovered that by allowing certain people to see my scars, I became a more real and approachable person. Without trying I can be quite intimidating. But by giving others a look at my scars,

I've discovered that people—women in particular—are less intimidated. By getting their own glimpse into the real me, the imperfect me, I make headway. I learned to use my scars. Early in my career, if I had a big meeting with an executive, I would wear short-sleeves. I wasn't playing the "sympathy card." All I was doing was attempting to find acceptance and level the playing field in the business world. By allowing people to see the "real" me, I felt I stood a better chance. Today, I wear my scars like a battle wound and no longer feel the need to expose or hide them.

My father grew up in a privileged home in the south. The name VanBibber meant something and he was expected to live up to it. His father, an astute businessman, was cruel to his children and the seeds of his abuse would carry on through my father's life and into mine. My father was a violent, abusive alcoholic and he often abused my mother. When he drank, he beat her, screamed at her, and humiliated her for any slight infraction, real or imagined. I have many memories of her sitting in the tub and watching it fill with her blood after these incidents. A few times, she attempted to leave. On one occasion, we'd made it out of the driveway and onto the road. My father ran from the house, jumping onto the hood of the car, screaming, "Let me in or I'll break the window!" My mother firmly told us, "Do not open the doors."

The fear was unimaginable, and I did something that to this day rips my soul apart: I opened the door. My father seized the opportunity and jumped into the car. From there he thrust my mother's head into the window. I can still see the blood and shattered glass; I can hear her screams. From the earliest age, I felt that it was my responsibility to protect her, yet on this occasion and so many others, I could not; I was just a little girl.

Many other times, my father took crazy to a whole new level. Flying his plane drunk and dive-bombing our house, he'd barely miss the power lines. I was helpless as neighbors came out to watch the spectacle. These outrageous events were embarrassing and I often found myself surrounded by concerned, yet amused neighbors. During these episodes, that was the time I began to embrace the notion of finding humor in tragedy. It's a trait that has served me well throughout my life.

I often tried to get between my parents when my father was violent. My every instinct focused on protecting my mother. I hoped that if I could somehow interrupt the cycle or redirect his anger, my mother would be spared. These efforts rarely worked, and I found myself helpless as I watched my mother bloodied at the hands of this man. My heart still breaks when I think of my mother and the abuse she endured. I hope her next life is better.

My brother also experienced the nightmare of growing up in an abusive home. However, when our father attacked our mother, my brother's instinct was always to hide. I fully understand that each of us, when faced with trauma, will handle it in a different way. There is no wrong or right way, there is only survival and in my young mind, the only survival I saw was protecting my mother.

I have many memories, some good and some not. There are many I've forgotten, hidden in a place my mind protects. Like so many children, I adored Santa Claus, and my mother always ensured that the holidays were special. One Christmas Eve, I awoke to some noise and sat bolt upright, believing that Santa must be at our house. I was quite sure that I heard sleigh bells and the movement of packages. I snuck into the living room to take a peek. It wasn't Santa. It was yet another horror scene from my shameful, painful family life; my father had my mother up against the closet. He held a gun to her head. As always, I ran to her, to protect her. Thankfully it worked and he did not pull the trigger. I may have been small, but I was strong when it came to protecting my mother. That gun, once owned by my grandmother, then my father, was passed down to me. For many years it sat in my safe and one day, I took full ownership of that gun by taking it into a local pawn shop and selling it. The owner informed me of the value and did his best to convince me to sell it to a collector, I simply looked at him and said, "You don't understand."

Looking back on those awful years, I'm struck by how I never feared for myself around my father, or that he might hurt *me*. My instinct to protect my mother was so incredibly fierce, nothing else mattered. I never let his size, power, or anger rule me; I was mighty and powerful in my own right. I now realize that the strength I mastered as a child is what led to my success as an adult.

The above accounts for battery, but physical trauma did not stop there. By the time I was four, my father had started sneaking into my bedroom and sexual abuse was layered atop all the other sources of pain and shame. His own childhood legacy of abuse was now playing out, in real time and in my life. It's a sad cycle, yet it is a fact: Children who endure abuse often grow up to abuse others. I know I am not alone; there are thousands of young girls and boys who fall victim to sexual predators and many of those are family members. I feared I would be like him as an adult. Every day I am grateful the abuse ended with him. My children were never exposed to such pain and I couldn't be more proud of the way they have turned out.

Back then, amidst the chaos of our daily lives, we experienced two tragedies. Ironically, these experiences gave me a break from my father's abuse. First, my father's fifty-four-year old mother, my much-adored grandmother, Iris, was killed in a head-on collision with a semi. I was nine at the time. Two years later, my father's sister, my beloved aunt Rhonda LaVon, lost control of her car and went off into a deep canyon. She was just twenty-four. I was devastated by the loss of these two dynamic women. Each woman was bigger than life, and until their untimely deaths, they'd enjoyed life to the fullest. They rode wild horses, drove fast cars, traveled the world and both had the man of their dreams in their lives.

My grandmother and aunt had shown quite an interest in me; my time with them was heaven on earth. With no friends at school and a household filled with pain and chaos, these women were my saviors. Just the year before, my grandmother took me for the summer. We traveled to Texas, Oklahoma and New Mexico. On several occasions, she would stop to visit a friend and ride one of their horses.

Like my mother, my paternal grandmother could ride and do most anything well. I remember the day she took me to a pueblo and bought me a little leather purse and a coin purse made of beads. I'd never owned anything that nice. To this day, I still have them tucked away where I keep all special things. Many times in my life, I've looked toward the sky, cried out their names, and begged for their help. I know they were a big part of my survival and I can still feel the warmth of their presence and feel that both will be my spirit guides.

One Act of Kindness, One Changed Life

As I got older, I learned to live with isolation at school and beyond. In those days, abuse was considered a private family affair and neighbors looked the other way. They also shunned us. Kids at school wrote the letters "CP" on the backs of their hands with black marker—"Cootie Protection"—in case they had the misfortune of accidentally brushing up against me as we passed in the hall. I didn't have a friend in the world. Not even one.

But one adult took a kind interest in me. She helped change my life, and the memory of her kindness remains with me to this day. She was my fifth-grade teacher, Mrs. Stuffle. She too was teased by classmates, taunted for her named and called Snuffleupagus. Admittedly, it was almost a relief to see my classmates' unkindness directed at someone else. Still, I began to feel protective of our teacher, and we bonded in a way that remains a cherished part of my life.

Mrs. Stuffle introduced me to the world of books and to the delights of reading. She must have seen my intelligence and thirst for learning that no other teacher or child in my school had noticed. Somehow, she looked past the tough but vilified little girl, past the scars and the isolation, and saw a spark within that she could help ignite. One day, after school, she lent me a book and let me take it home to read, and from that day on, I never stopped reading.

My time with Mrs. Stuffle was actually the postscript to my learned love of reading. A couple years earlier, when I was in the third grade, I'd been crazy about a book series. I became attached to the characters, one of whom happened to be African American, and they felt like my only true friends. Spot the dog, his owner, and friends were so vivid and real. I brought the book home. Happily lost in it, my father ruined the entire experience by angrily snatching the book from my hands. He screamed that no daughter of his was permitted to read a book with a black character in it, though he used a cruder word. The next day, he marched me into the principal's office and slammed the book on the desk. Going forward, I was not allowed story time with my classmates or the treasure of bringing a book home. Two years would pass before I touched another book.

So when Mrs. Stuffle placed a carefully selected book in my hands, one that she thought was perfect for a ten-year-old girl, it was like drinking cool, fresh water after wandering in the desert. It was freedom. The book she loaned me was *Little House on the Prairie*. Like so many children, I fell under the spell of Laura Ingalls Wilder's bewitching storytelling. Interestingly and sadly, my father allowed this book because all the characters were white.

After I read the book, Mrs. Stuffle actually wanted to hear whether I liked it or not. I blurted out how much I loved it, making a first tiny, tenuous connection with someone outside my family, trusting someone with a little glimpse, however small, into my real self. It sounds like such a small thing, but it meant so much. It was the start of something beautiful and for anyone lucky enough to have a teacher take them under their wing, blessings are certain to unfold.

It became clear to my teacher that I hungered for the mind-opening experiences that books brought to my mean and narrow life, and she directed me to more and more and more books. Mrs. Stuffle expanded my horizons in other ways, too. She let me stay after school to take on special projects. I felt valued and useful, and I saw that I had gifts to offer, even if no one else would recognize them. I was smart, after all, and I could solve problems and complete special work that others in the class did not experience.

Like every kid, especially those looking to escape painful and abusive home lives, I daydreamed. I had only three means of escape. One was to jump on my bike for a sweet, if temporary, reprieve from the dangers and chaos of our home. Another was losing myself in the world of the written word. And the last was to sit on the front porch of our home and dream big, if seemingly impossible, dreams. I believed with every ounce of my soul that those dreams would come true. Many years later, in my adult life, they did.

Reading books fed my imagination and fueled those daydreams. My dreams seemed so remote and so unattainable in those days. I wanted a home that was safe, I wanted children who knew they had their mother's love and protection. I wanted a successful career and to touch the lives of others, making a real difference in peoples' lives. I wanted to be far away from my loud and dangerous home and be surrounded by the trusting, loving presence of animals in a peaceful place in the country.

I had one additional activity in my world that provided the perfect escape—Girl Scouts. I was obsessed with filling my badge and the one night of meetings each week meant I could get away from home. My mother introduced me to scouting at an early age, yet she left it up to me to excel at it. I found, at this tender age, that I had the ability to work hard and earn achievements. I found I had hidden talents and although I may not have fit the "mold" of the common Girl Scout, I was bound and determined to be the best at it. To this day I have my sash, with all those badges so hard won. I know that in those early childhood efforts lay the stepping stones of my adult success.

Whether it was Mrs. Stuffle's influence, my scout master's tutelage, a natural born drive, or all the preceding, believing I could do something bigger than myself was a respite—it provided hope. Dreaming planted seeds in me. They would lay dormant for a little longer as I continued to endure the rocky soil of life.

A Stolen Childhood

My father sexually abused me. As so many abusers do, he made it clear that this was a shameful secret, that it was all my fault, and that I would be rejected by everyone—my mother included—if I ever breathed a word to anyone. I know I speak for many children when I say it's difficult to describe just how helpless a child feels in these situations, where the balance of power is so completely one-sided. You have nowhere to run, nowhere to hide, and no one to listen. You are completely alone.

Throughout my life, I've experienced many different layers of abuse, including physical and sexual abuse at the hands of my father. I've grown to believe that those with abusive personalities know how to identify children who are vulnerable. It's almost like you have a sign on your back that predators can see that's invisible to healthy, normal people. They find you, they know you're vulnerable, and they exploit that. I've attracted many abusers, not because of my own actions, but because I believe an abused child develops an aura that pedophiles and sick beasts can detect and that they are all too eager to exploit.

At one point, three teenage boys began to stalk me. They took me to their basement and abused me again and again. They said that if I ever told anyone, no matter when and no matter where I was, they would find me and do to me what they did to others—unspeakable acts.

I have lived with that fear my entire life, that they would find me and I would pay. It was embedded in the very core, animal part of my brain. When I look back on my life, I see how this terrible fear of being hunted down, being killed, had I ever spoken out, clouded everything. This included my career, my relationships, and my life choices. That horrifying experience was also the reason I never penned this book—until now.

What my father and those boys down the street did to me stole my childhood in many ways. There was no room to feel safe, no years of innocence, no growing into my sexuality as a loving and exploring experience, no control of my own destiny.

As dreams go, I lived off one that differed from the escape of my angry violent world, and my biggest dream was that my father would leave. My mother, my brother, and my new baby sister, Audra, and I could live freely with him gone. When my father finally abandoned us, that dream came true. However, one thing I did not foresee was how my role within my family would change. I was about to become a parent to my two younger siblings and on that day my childhood vanished forever.

From Haves to Have-Nots

I was twelve years old when my father left us. I vividly remember the joy and relief I felt. He was gone! We could finally live like "normal" people, and laugh and smile and make noise whenever we wanted! My mother would no longer endure savage beatings, and I would no longer cringe in my room at night, praying that my father would not come sit on my bed, his breath stinking of alcohol and his hands and body intruding, probing, hurting, taking away what precious little remained of my privacy and self-worth.

This is the reason I was so confused by my mother's reaction when my father left. My brother was ten and my baby sister was two months. We had so much time ahead of us! But instead of sharing my joy and liberation, my mother sat down and cried. This woman was strong, yet she felt helpless. This was in the '70s when many women had limited choices in life. Although, at one point, my mother enjoyed a great career as a makeup artist, a job my father made her give up. Also, she never finished college. In truth, she may have never left him. That's why it was such a blessing when he left us.

I felt lost and hopeless. For all that she had endured at the hands of my father, my mother *never* cried. She screamed, sobbed and begged, but she never simply cried. As children, we watched with fear and confusion. In my memory, even baby Audra seemed to know that something was wrong. I just couldn't comprehend my mother's behavior. I wanted to jump up and down and shout, "Why are you crying? He's gone! We're free!"

Days before he left, my father had convinced my mother to go to Wisconsin, taking us with her for the weekend. He told her he'd picked out a nice little resort where we would stay.

"You can relax with the kids for a couple of days, and then I'll come up and join you."

The two days came and went, but my father never arrived. From my perspective, every moment that he wasn't around was a stolen moment of safety, so I didn't think much about it. But my mother grew anxious, alternating between worried and frightened. Finally, she bundled us up and we piled in the car and headed home. I can only imagine the thoughts that raced through her mind when she walked into our house—only to find it completely empty.

It turned out there was more than just the empty house. My father had sold the land that our new home was going to be built on—it was supposed to be our dream home—big enough for our newly expanded family. He'd taken the plane and cars; all that was left was my mother's car and the possessions we'd brought with us for our "family vacation."

We had no furniture, toys, or clothes. The bank accounts were empty. My mother was left alone with three children. Instead of a family which, for all its problems, was prosperous and moving up in the world, we were now totally destitute.

As far as we could see, he had disappeared from the face of the earth. He simply vanished. In those pre-Internet days, it was much easier for someone who didn't want to be found to stay hidden and he had the added support of his family. The mechanisms for tracking down an absentee parent and getting child support were not very sophisticated. In the end, we never got a penny. From that moment on, my mother had to do it all alone.

I went from "have" to "have not" overnight. Ever since then, I've always been keenly aware that the line between a comfortable life and one of grinding hunger and poverty is thin. We are all just one or two bad breaks away from finding ourselves in an unthinkable situation. You can cross that line so easily and never see it coming—and not be able to stop it even if you did see it coming. To this day, the specters of poverty and hunger terrify me.

In that time period following my father's disappearance, I became a parent to my brother and sister, while my mother put every ounce of her energy into earning a living, attending college, and keeping a roof over our heads, as well as food in our bellies. In those moments, I crossed into adulthood.

My grandmother, Iris

My aunt Rhonda LaVon, riding

My father, age 20, working for one of the
VanBibber family-owned business

*Photo of my mother taken during the
Miss Arkansas Pageant*

My brother, Mark Winston VanBibber, and me

My father, age 20

My aunt Rhonda LaVon, age 14

My mother, Aunt Rhonda LaVon and me

My grandmother, Iris, with her son, Don, and daughter, Rhonda LaVon

Mother, son and daughter, soon to be on their own

Our family home

Girl Scouts — "My Great Escape"

My parents, 1964

My brother and me

Rare family photo

CHAPTER TWO

Fighting Forward

Crafting a lie is so time-consuming
Pitching reality against my fantasy world did me no good
My "dream" world was so pretty, white fences and cloud-filled skies
I had all the lies memorized, stored right here...they became my truth
Years passed and my truth became my reality
Waking, sleeping, talking, and walking, I had all the answers memorized
Who suspected, who had doubts? Oh no, I have fooled them all
Soon, I was up against the wall—forgetting the fabric of this reality
Falling deeper into lies. I had to own my truth, my story, my me
For this was the only way for me to walk free

Every day was a fight to keep food on the table, a roof over our heads, and clothing on our backs. My days were a blur: getting my younger siblings ready for school or daycare, getting us to our respective destinations, then getting everyone back home again so I could get dinner on the table. My mom was in school full-time to earn her degree. She needed to make enough money to keep the wolf from the door. I am proud to say my mom was one tough lady. She went on to graduate with double honors.

Meanwhile, everything was scarce: time, money, food, patience. I had to do everything within my power to contribute financially. My brother and I took on two paper routes to bring in a few extra dollars. I had never really cooked before, and now I was tasked with preparing breakfast and dinner every weekday. At school I was a greater outcast than ever. On top of everything, I was now the kid who bore the mark of scandal—a father who'd abandoned his family. I also carried the stink and stigma of complete poverty.

Poverty drove me to extremes. Out of desperation, I became an adept shoplifter. As kids, we were always hungry, and I didn't want to further burden my mother. In the winter, I would wade through the deep bone-chilling snows of northern Illinois to walk to the grocery store. I'd wear my big coat and fill its deep pockets with food for myself, my brother and my sister. It was a two-mile walk to the store, but there was no other way to get enough food in our bellies.

I could fit quite a bit of food in the nooks and crannies of my coat. It was shameful to steal—and it was scary. I wasn't frightened by the store managers; I was frightened by my mother. If I was caught stealing it would result in a sound and painful beating from her.

At times, I had so much food in my coat that I couldn't walk all the way home with the heavy load. On the way home, near the abandoned mining pits, I'd found a little hiding spot. It was a good place for me to stash food, and I would return later to pick it up.

I was always afraid when I returned to the hiding spot. I wasn't the only kid doing bad things and using an off-limits area. A group of older boys used that area for all sorts of bad things, and I was terrified of crossing their paths. Just the year before, the body of a young girl was found in the mining pits. I was acutely aware that my life was in danger in this abandoned place. I was always mindful and extra careful not to be seen, avoiding those boys at all costs.

On one occasion, I thought the coast was clear. I was retrieving my stash when I heard the boys' voices. I jumped into the nearest bushes and crouched, praying they wouldn't see me. I was certain that my heart pounded so loud that they would hear it. I was terrified of two things. If discovered, what awful "fun" might they have at my expense? Secondly, I feared they'd find my stash of food. I got lucky that day, but the memory of those petrifying, slow-passing moments remains with me decades later.

I had to be resourceful in other ways, and soon I was dragging my wagon around the neighborhood collecting empty pop bottles from the neighbors. After that came the two-mile trek to the store to get the penny-per-bottle refund. If my bottle haul was large enough, and my earnings big enough, I could buy that much more food.

The humiliating mix of pity and disdain—something neighbors barely bothered to disguise—was a deep source of shame. The entire community regarded my family as an embarrassment, as if we were a stain on this proper, upright Midwestern community. However, I never let fear or humiliation hold me back. I did what I had to in order to survive. While others may have viewed me as a beggar, I taught myself to think of it as business. I was working, using the few resources I had, plus my own wits, to provide for my family.

Other than riding my bike or daydreaming during a few stolen moments on the front porch, I had one other source of escape. My father had always loved listening to saxophonist Boots Randolph, and I grew to love him. In sixth grade, all the students had an opportunity to choose an instrument and join the school band. It seemed preordained that I would pick the saxophone. Although I was small in stature, I chose the larger, heavier tenor sax over the lighter alto sax; I just loved the way the soulful tenor sax sounded and the beautiful range it covered.

Solace in Music

I viewed my band director, Karen Vanni, with admiration and fear. She was tough. She made me memorize many of my pieces—no reading from the sheet music. Every single day I lugged that heavy saxophone home and tucked it safely in my bedroom. Every chance I got, I'd shut my door and practice that sax until my lips bled. It was my escape from fear, abuse, and responsibility. At times, I think that saxophone was the only thing that kept me alive.

Miss Vanni appreciated how hard I pushed myself and the musical progress I made. She seemed to understand the most precious moments of my school day was the solace I found in her band room. She also recognized that my fighting, competitive spirit would serve me well in my determination to master my instrument. She started entering me in contests, and I threw myself into the music and the competitive world with everything I had. By the eighth grade I was attending competitions near and far, and doing well. Through it all, my mother made some incredible sacrifices. This was to ensure I had a quality instrument that would allow me to compete at a high level. But what Miss Vanni did also helped save my life. She opened a door I had never entered, and for the very first time, I felt pride in my accomplishments. She took a troubled child and made her into a champion.

My mother's brother, Larry Kurtz, an officer in the Navy, came to visit. My mother adored her younger brother and she had an idea about how to make him happy. She planned on introducing him to Miss Vanni. We all attended a softball game that Miss Vanni was coaching and the connection between her and my uncle seemed immediate. The next year, they were married. For me this was such a blessing and thrill—my beloved and well-respected Uncle Larry was marrying a woman who had brought light into my life. I remain grateful for their union; it brought me three incredible cousins. This includes my cousin, Tracey Kurtz. She means the world to me. To this day, I can pick up the phone to chat about anything and everything with her. I'm so fortunate to have a special cousin who is also a trusted friend.

Somewhere along the way, I acquired what was one of my proudest possessions: a pair of shiny white vinyl go-go boots. At a time when so many of my clothes were shabby and second-hand, I loved those boots fiercely. The boots represented possibility, a potential ticket to popularity and friendship. When I wore the boots, I was sure the other girls at school would want to get to know me!

Shortly after I got the boots, I was taking some pot pies out of the oven—a tried and true recipe my mom taught me—when I lost control of the baking sheet. One of the pot pies plopped right down inside my beautiful boot. The hot filling stuck to my skin and the burn was painful. I can still see my sister and brother's bewildered faces—Audra in her high chair and Mark at the table—as I leapt around the kitchen, screaming in pain.

It seemed outrageous and so unfair that more pain and disappointment could be piled onto my young life. Today, surprisingly, I look back on it and am able to find the humor in so many things. It's easy to laugh when I recall jumping around the kitchen, much like a chicken, and just how silly I must have appeared to my siblings; I've continued to find humor in even the darkest of times in my life. As a friend once told me: "Laugh you live, cry you die."

Goodbye to School Days

Eventually, it became clear that the paper route and pop bottles would not bring in enough money to fill the gaps. I took a job working in a diner. That was okay during the summer when I had time. But when the school year rolled around and I started ninth grade the job was overwhelming. I couldn't fit it all in—full-time caregiver to my siblings, full-time wage earner, and full-time student. Something had to give. I made the decision to leave school and focus on work. I dropped out; it would become yet another shameful thing I'd spend a lifetime hiding.

I didn't discuss giving up school with anyone. I just made my decision and quit. Initially, the school called the house to check on me. I did a great job of pretending to be my mother, then I would go on to give some pretext of why I was out that day. Eventually I told them, "Celia won't be coming back." From there, I moved on with my life the best way I knew how.

My mother was stretched thin with her studies and with the burden of single parenting; she was often short-tempered and impatient. Like many victims of abuse, the cycle began to repeat, and she turned to brute force when she didn't know how to get through to us. I grew to expect savage beatings if I disappointed her or dropped the ball on one of my growing responsibilities. To be honest, I did my fair share of acting out, rule breaking, all of which caused my mother a great deal of anguish.

After one particularly brutal beating, I ended up in the emergency room. I had a drape over my face and the only exposed area was the skin being stitched back together. I heard footsteps, people entering the room. They started asking questions about my injury. Was this an accident? How did it happen? Did someone hurt me, and if so, what were their names? I laid there terrified. I could never "out" my mother, or be the reason our family was displaced. I was thankful for the drape covering my eyes. The people questioning me wouldn't see the telltale signs of a girl who was lying, and lie I did.

Shortly after this incident, I began to understand that I needed to get away from the house. This was not only to protect my own life, but to stop being a destructive nuisance at home. I was acting out and the result of my behavior was stern discipline. I realized I was causing my mother more stress and the beatings were a direct result of my behaviors. My heart broke to think of being physically separated from my siblings, but I couldn't see any other way. When I was well enough, I took a bus across town and marched into the juvenile detention center. I told them that I refused to go home because I feared for my life. They tried to get me to go back, stating they had no evidence that my home environment was unsafe, but I flatly refused. I persisted, telling them they could put me in the juvenile detention center if need be. I would not return home. That was how I entered the foster care system.

The Revolving Door

My first foster experience took place at a beautiful home in the country. My foster parents were an older couple with a young son, and we passed our days in the country way: wandering the woods, shooting chipmunks, getting lost in cornfields and enjoying the outdoor deck. Even though these foster parents were good to me, I could never allow myself to feel safe. I slept each night with the covers tucked tightly from head to toe, like a coat of armor between the world and me. The habit continued until I was twenty-three, long after my foster-care days. I think the family grew fearful when they realized how damaged I was. Evidently, I talked in my sleep. Eventually, my foster parents put a monitor next to my bed, listening. I don't know what they heard, but soon after that I was taken, with no explanation, from their home. As the caseworker loaded me into the car, the pain and rejection was almost more than I could bear.

The next family had five foster children, in addition to their own three kids. In this home, the foster children were housed in the dank basement. We slept on mattresses while the parents and their children occupied the upstairs. Every Sunday the family would cook a week-long supply of burgers. During the week, the foster children ate the burgers while the family dined on steaks and other delicious food. We'd look on, but kept our mouths shut. Even worse, the "father" enjoyed having the teenage girls sit on his lap, and it made my stomach somersault when it was my turn.

While I was with this family, the caseworkers enrolled me in school again. Thankfully, I tested out of the ninth grade, and picked back up with the tenth-grade curriculum. It was strange to be back in school, though once again I was the outsider. On an up note, a different band director had a kind heart, and took an interest in a lost girl who was clearly ostracized by her peers. Over time, we began conversing in his office. When the band director came to understand my current plight in foster care, he and his wonderful wife contacted child services. Once I was removed from that hell hole, the band director and his wife took me in, where I was welcomed by them and their two young daughters.

Finally, I was in a supportive home where I could play my beloved saxophone. I had plenty to eat and quiet time to do my homework. I loved my new "little sisters." Coincidentally, at the same time, my mother started allowing visits with my own sister, Audra. Each day, when Audra was dropped off, was a true thrill. The time I spent with her and the band director's girls was precious. We played for hours, read books, and climbed trees.

Unfortunately, tragedy struck again, and my own dark past betrayed me. A monitor had been placed in the bedroom. At some point, my new foster parents heard me talking in my sleep. When I woke up they peppered me with questions which I couldn't answer. They needed to protect their own two daughters and arranged for me to leave. They did the right thing; we must all protect our children. I never have learned what secrets I shared in my sleep, and I consider it a blessing that I don't remember.

I completed only a few months in the tenth grade after testing out of the ninth. I never returned to formal schooling, but when I was sixteen I took the GED. I entered the testing room terrified, wondering how I could pass this test with only an eighth-grade education. I was sure I would fail.

Yet I had to try—a GED would open up job opportunities. Thankfully, I passed with flying colors.

Back at Home

I was sent back to my mother, who had recently received her degree in accounting. I remember the pride I felt sitting in the audience and hearing her name spoken with the added elements of "double honors." How she did that, with three children, was truly unbelievable. She found work quickly and would eventually open her own firm. I looked for full-time work to help provide for Mark and Audra. I lied about my age and managed to get a job in the local nursing home. I took third shift so my mother could drop me off and pick me up. It was necessary to work around her schedule and my siblings' school days. By this point, my mother knew I had dropped out of school and that battle was a done deal.

I loved caring for the nursing home residents. Some of them had developed decubitus ulcers, painful skin sores from being left in the same position in bed for too long. I would carefully tend to their wounds and turn them over every couple of hours, helping and healing people who couldn't help or heal themselves. Sadly, there were many things that weren't right in this nursing home: filthy conditions, inadequate care, the nutrition. The food they expected these people to eat was appalling. It broke my heart and I did all that I could, everything within my power, to make a difference. Eventually, I took a bold chance and reported the nursing home abuses. Then I left my job and got work at another nursing home. I grew to love the residents as if they were family, and I was determined to protect them.

Many nursing home residents never had any visitors, so I sat and talked with them for hours. For once, I was someone who others wanted to spend time with. I can still see their faces and hear their stories. One wonderful woman was very kind; she and I would converse for hours. She gave me a book about the life of Lauren Bacall. I was instantly addicted to Bacall's fascinating and extraordinary life. It began a new trend in my life; I've never stopped reading about strong women. Their tragedies and triumphs fill my mind, and hearing their stories is one of my very great pleasures. I am sure this woman in the nursing home had no idea how that small gesture would impact my life. Things like this are reminders of how our lives are often changed by kind gestures.

Since school was no longer a question, I got other day jobs. Among these was a job on a coffee truck, delivering coffee, and cleaning coffee makers at local businesses. I began to notice our customers' attire, the neatly arranged desks and, of course, personalized coffee cups. There was something about an office environment that I found appealing. I felt a tug deep down inside that said, "One day, this will be me." All was well until the company owner made a pass at me. I thought, "Really? I'm working hard and doing all you ask, yet you find it necessary to degrade me?" I refused to go back to the nightmare of abuse—so I quit.

My next job was at a cafeteria style restaurant, primarily frequented by the elderly. Once again, I was surrounded by people with colorful histories, elaborate stories, and old jokes. When it was slow, I would steal what minutes I could to sit down and chat with these remarkable people. The uniform required me to wear a white dress and shoes. The only pair of white shoes I could afford were made of cheap plastic and one size too small. But I needed that job, so I plunked down my six dollars for the shoes and didn't look back. Each day was a struggle to shove my feet into those shoes. I used oil, baby powder, or Crisco to assist in putting them on my feet. Despite my painful, swollen feet, I loved my job and all the people who generously shared their stories. I did not have a car and many times there was no ride available, so I'd walk. My painful feet were a reminder of just how much I loved my sister and brother, and what I'd do to care for them. The experience made me a stronger person.

Always in survival mode, at the end of my shift I'd cram my pockets with desserts for Mark and Audra. In those lean years, we never had desserts. They absolutely loved it when I came home with these treats. I can still remember looking down at my feet, throbbing and swollen, then glancing up to see their precious faces all lit up as they ate and ate until their bellies were satisfied. At that moment, I felt it was all worth it.

It was during this time that I began to attract the eye of a few young men. I accepted a date here and there, when I could spare the time. Yet, I never allowed myself the freedom of entering into a relationship. I did not possess the ability to care for another person, at least not one outside of my immediate family. Those unfortunate enough to enjoy a date with me usually found there would not be a second, I was either too busy or simply not interested. Regardless of my insecurities, I was beginning to develop a social life and my circle of friends was growing. I began paying more attention to my looks. Makeup and hair now became important to me and I made time for my friends in a way I hadn't done in the past. I was crawling out of my shell and it all felt real good.

Forgiveness

This book would not be complete if it did not share the strongest message I can give to anyone reading: forgiveness.

I remember sitting with my therapist when I was in my teens. It wasn't my first visit; in fact, I'd been seeing him for several months. From the beginning, he probed me with questions regarding my lack of childhood memories and I told him, "I have no memories before the age of twelve." Years later, in future counseling, I would recall many of those dark days, not all, but enough to share in this memoir.

I thought no one had memories before that age. It seemed perfectly normal to me, and for the life of me, I couldn't figure out why he kept revisiting this subject. He gently told me about the memories that most children have, and he explained what was normal and what was not. A piece of me shattered, for in that moment, I knew. I didn't know what I knew—yet, but I had a sense of forbidden knowledge.

As our time together progressed, the therapist was successful in resurrecting small bits of my memories, buried so deep and secret that even in this safe environment, I eluded him with stories of my make-believe world and some of those memories are shared here, in this book.

My counseling ended. I tucked away the knowledge that I was once again broken, for who doesn't remember their childhood? It would be many years before I had the answers, and many answers are simply not worth knowing.

Moving on a number of years, as an adult I became a licensed real estate agent. During that time, I played very hard and on one occasion, I had a physical altercation with my sister, Audra. The large diamond and amethyst ring on my finger hit her chin and I was an immediate mess of regret and shame. How could I hit her, my baby, the love of my life? What was wrong with me, I needed to find out.

The next day, I checked myself into a high-dollar, thirty-day vacation "villa" of sorts. Shortly into my stay, my therapist suggested I undergo sodium amytal therapy. At the time, the drug was used to access past relevant memories, most specifically from childhood. I agreed to undergo the treatment, and the date was set.

I remember nothing of that experience. I was later told that the drug typically works within minutes, exposing memories long forgotten. Yet for me, it took nearly two hours. Interestingly, the medical staff in charge shared that I was very good at evading questions and creating fabricated responses, even after being sedated with this powerful drug. I took them on long journeys of a history that made no sense and at some point, I finally began to tell the truth. The entire session was taped. Over the next several weeks, my therapist and I cautiously listened to and dissected the memories I had shared. I know the memories were facts—true events, but to this day I cannot speak about them in detail.

With this new knowledge, my therapist suggested I call one of my abusers—my father—and confront him. The next day we did just that. To my horror, he denied everything. I worked through this, left the facility days later, and never looked back. The tapes are still mine, tucked safely away, and I will never listen to them again. Protecting my mind and my heart from the past is vital to my survival.

When I was thirty years old and pregnant with my daughter, Hillary, an interesting event occurred. My father called at 4:30 in the morning. He said that he needed to talk, and I said I was happy to listen. He began by telling me that he was remembering things from long ago. He revisited, in great detail, the many times he sexually abused me. I was thankful to have my growing belly to touch for support and strength, for my heart was breaking. After twenty minutes, I asked my father, "Did you burn me?"

His response was an immediate, "NO!" In that moment, I realized that it didn't matter whether he had a memory of burning me or not. Yet I replied to his denial with the words, "I forgive you."

Over the next twenty-one years we exchanged pleasant phone calls and the occasional card. There was the occasional visit, such as the time I drove to Arkansas and visited him while he was in a treatment facility for alcohol addiction. Then, in 2005, my father rang me and said he'd be coming though Texas on his way to Guatemala for some fishing. He wanted to stop by my ranch to pay a visit. As the day grew closer, I asked myself, "Did you really forgive him? What are you going to feel when you see him?" Had I simply been giving lip service to forgiveness?

I remember that day clearly. His truck, towing his fishing rig, slowly scaled my long drive. I took a deep breath, perhaps the deepest of my life, and walked out the door. I forced a smile. As I approached my father, the only thing I felt was the love of a daughter for her father. I hugged him long and hard. It was one of the best moments of my life.

Forgiveness is a tricky thing. We can say the word and never believe the word. Yet, for those of us blessed enough to truly experience the act of forgiveness, it's an overwhelming sense of joy. Does it come from God? This I don't know. What I do know is that my father never wanted to hurt me. He was a troubled child in a man's body. To this day, I love him, respect him, and cherish each phone call, card, and visit.

We all have the ability to forgive. It's an act and a choice that makes us stronger, kinder, and wiser.

Band Camp, I am seen here, second row, far right

Last photo of Mark and me with our father

School photo of Audra

My brother and me

Uncle Larry with my brother and me

My aunt, Karen Vanni, along with
my mother

Pictured here with my beloved
Super Action 80 Selmer tenor sax

My mother finally allowed Audra to visit me at my
foster home. A day filled with joy

Finally, I begin to develop a group of friends

Early dating

My mother, graduating from college

Visiting my father during one of his stays in rehab

Chapter Three
Survival

I live in a house called torture and pain
It's made of materials called sorrow and shame
It's a horrid place in which to dwell, with a wicked room which some call hell
From the faucets run my tears, cried by me for many years,
But, the worst part to face—is this place, for the best of me will die here,
perish without a chance...all alone

A Survivor

My brother was ten, my sister two months, and I was twelve when our father left us. I felt the responsibilities and burdens of an adult and, in many ways, I felt more like a parent than a sibling to Mark and Audra. I was fiercely protective of my siblings, especially baby Audra, but I think at an unconscious level I resented the responsibility. Even though I was still a child, I was raised to be tough—physically and emotionally—and I rose to meet challenge after challenge.

For many years, I felt personally responsible for every trial or struggle Mark or Audra faced, even into their adulthoods. I worried that I hadn't raised them well enough or set a strong enough example when they were young. Although I no longer faced the day-in, day-out struggles, such as getting food, making sure they were washed, dressed, and ready for school each day, I couldn't escape the ongoing feeling of responsibility for their decisions and their lives. I felt wholly accountable.

I discussed this with my therapist as I began the work of reconciling my inner and outer lives. I rehashed details of how I handled various episodes with Mark and Audra when we were all children, second-guessing whether I'd made a wrong choice or failed them in some fundamental way. I was cruel to my brother, and to this day I am haunted by those instances.

By the grace of God, Mark turned out really well. After his military stint, he went on to enjoy an exciting career in the Middle East. His work takes him to Saudi Arabia, Bahrain, the United Arab Emirates, and other exotic locations. He lives in Cyprus with his beautiful Scottish wife, Tricia. He speaks thirteen languages and is in high demand in his field. He found his own form of survival and I hope he knows how proud I am of him.

I vividly remember a critical turning point. My therapist held up his hand, looked me deep in the eyes and said, "Celia, you were only a child, and a child should never be expected to raise children."

As his words sank in, I looked back at my relationship with Mark and Audra with a new perspective. I was just a child and I did the best I could with what resources I had. I now regard them as a loving sister and brother, accepting that they make their own decisions as independent adults, just as I make my own decisions. I've been able to stand with Audra and fight for her as she worked through her own addiction and depression issues. I helped her find the path to recovery. Audra went on to get her degree and joined my mother in her accounting practice. She also provides quite a bit of volunteer work with AA and NA, including being a sponsor to many people struggling with addiction. That said, her children and her grandchildren are the center of her world and she loves me, her "Sissy."

Through the years we struggled with zero financial or emotional support from our father. On occasion, he would drift into our lives. A brief visit, a post card from some distant country or a telephone call were all we had to mark our days as his children. Yet, each of us looked forward to any contact we had with him; he was after all, our father. He would arrive with much bravado and exit as quickly as he came. I don't know how my mother tolerated it. Perhaps she saw some measure of hope in our young eyes and in turn, that gave her hope. Yet, in the end, there was none.

My Shining Star

My childhood was not all sadness and pain, for I had a hero. My cousin, Keena Rothhammer, was a world class swimmer. Many of her meets were covered on television and I would sit breathless as I watched her take the block at meets far and wide. I adored her! One summer my mother packed my brother, my grandfather and myself in the car and drove to California to visit Keena, her brothers and my Aunt Dianne at their sprawling home in the desert. Keena was so kind to me, cleaning out her closet and "gifting" me several of her swim club jackets and memorabilia. The entire visit was surreal, I had never been in such a stunning home, with full time staff, a pool in the backyard and views of the mountains for miles. Our lives were polar opposites, yet here I was, sitting at a beautifully set table, eating meals prepared by well-organized staff and sleeping in a bed that felt like it belonged in heaven.

The next year my mother and I drove to Chicago to see Keena swim in the Olympic trials and not only did she qualify, but I had the opportunity to meet Mark Spitz, Shirley Babashoff and Shane Gould. Keena went on to compete in the Munich Olympics, setting two new world records and bringing home a gold and bronze medal. The following year she was named the North American Athlete of the year and went on to become a sports commentator at CBS. The pride I felt nearly burst my heart and I walked with a new sort of confidence. We all need a hero in our lives. They don't need to be Olympians or superheroes, a hero can be of your choosing or perhaps of God's.

Finally, A Friend

I didn't always carry the burden of surrogate parent gracefully. During our teen years, I often tormented Mark and became obsessed with the idea of getting him out of the house for good. Then I would have fewer responsibilities. At times, I was abusive toward Mark, playing forward that cycle of abuse that went from my father to my mother and from my mother to me. In our chaotic and crazy house, things could quickly swing from love and laughter to fear and intimidation. You never knew what was coming next. Each of us developed our own ways of coping with that struggle.

Finally, when I was fourteen, something changed for the better. For the first time in my life, I experienced the delicious joy of having a friend. Yes, a friend! Her name was Rhonda, and she brought the amazing roller coaster of teenage fun and friendship into my life, which had been so isolated until then. Rhonda was bigger than life, crazy and hilarious. One of the things about her I still cherish is that she had this amazing ability to wolf whistle. It became my calling card to freedom and fun. It was so loud, I heard her from two or three blocks away. How she managed to produce such a sound with her small hands amazed me. Whenever I heard that whistle, my heart would sing with joy. If I heard her whistle, I would run out the door and into the street to greet her. I never knew what Rhonda and I would be up to when we were together, but I knew it would be an adventure.

Rhonda was adopted by her great-aunt, and she was every bit as independent-minded as me. Together we were determined to live life at a fast and furious pace. Fun, trouble, and rock-and-roll were part of the fabric in our small Illinois town. Rhonda and I could play with the best of them, and we were fearless. As our friendship blossomed, we hung out with other kids. For the first time, I experienced the social swirl that more typical kids had always known.

Of course, I sometimes confided to Rhonda and my other friends how much I resented Mark. I considered him a killjoy tattletale. I would fantasize out loud about how I wished he would disappear from my life. Looking back, I agonize over the way I treated my brother.

One day we got the brilliant idea to pool our money and put him on a one-way bus. We went to the Greyhound station and bought a ticket to the farthest destination our resources could afford. Rhonda's family was gone for the day, so we took the keys to her aunt's car. She'd never driven before, so this heightened the thrill of the experience. As planned, we told Mark that he was going on an exciting adventure to see our father. He didn't seem at all suspicious that Rhonda was driving and that no adult seemed to be involved in this sudden adventure.

We were brilliant! We got Mark bundled onto the bus and held our breath until it pulled out of the station. We gleefully jumped up and down, impressed by how well our clever plan had worked. Oh, I was so bad! I was thrilled we had pulled this off. The little tattling brother was gone, gone, gone! I hung out with my friends for the rest of the day, laughing and lighthearted.

When I walked into the house that night, I was completely shocked to find Mark there, sitting on the sofa with a very odd expression on his face. My heart jumped up into my throat as I realized that not only had my plan failed, but by now my mother knew every detail. I was in for a one hell of a beating.

Her weapon of choice was the metal wand on our Filter Queen Vacuum, and I was well-acquainted with it. I dove into the closet and held onto the doorknob for dear life while my mother pulled hard on it from the other side. She was quite amped up, yanking on it with considerable strength and fury. I knew, all too well, the pain and injuries that metal wand could produce. I still carry the emotional and physical scars from the rage my mother unleashed that day. Now it seems funny to me, that we were fiercely tugging against each other through the closet door as I tried to escape the inevitable. Over the years, I've learned to find and enjoy the humor in these memories. I prefer to laugh at the absurdities, instead of dwelling on the pain.

In the long run, I actually did succeed in getting rid of my brother. When he was seventeen and I was nineteen, I convinced him to join the Navy. I talked to him about the adventures he'd have, how he would stand on his own two feet, how he could get away and see the world far beyond our little town. Ultimately, he enlisted. Of course, there's no turning back from a commitment to join the military. Despite my mother's objections, he was off on a three-year journey. My long-held wish came true.

As I previously mentioned, my brother turned out very well, considering the childhood he endured. In addition to speaking thirteen languages, he has lived in or visited ninety-seven countries and is considered one of the best experts in the world of aviation. He has seen all seven continents and all seven seas, he married the woman of his dreams, a tall, Scottish woman with the same gusto for life he possesses. He and I share a passion for living, perhaps because, as children, our passion was so many times comprised by violence and dysfunction.

Rebels

Whenever Rhonda and I were together, we got into our share of trouble. Rhonda's aunt/adopted mother and my mother tried to talk some sense into us, but it only made us more rebellious. We were hell-bent on fun and trouble.

One cold winter day, Rhonda and I decided we'd go find her birth mother in Shellsburg, Iowa. Being teens and acting as teens often do, it was an impulsive decision. We thought it would be a grand adventure and a way of spreading our wings and asserting our independence. Selfishly, we didn't give a single thought to the pain and confusion our disappearance would cause our families.

We broke open our piggy banks and counted our loot. Filled with anticipation, we shoved a few clothes into our bags and headed to the Greyhound station. Sure enough, we had just enough for two one-way tickets to Cedar Rapids. Just sitting on that bus was an incredible adventure; it was dangerous and exhilarating. After the first couple of hours, we crossed the Illinois line and entered Iowa. We felt so grown-up and worldly traveling by ourselves to places we'd never seen!

It was well after dark when we got to the bus station in Cedar Rapids. As we stepped out into the freezing cold, realization set in. We still needed to get to the town where Rhonda's birth mother lived. Shellsburg was about an hour away from where we were. Being two ill-equipped, uneducated teens, we stuck our thumbs out—and sure enough, after a while, a car pulled over and the driver offered us a warm ride. Fortunately, the guy who picked us up was friendly enough and we chatted animatedly.

Perhaps he was showing off to two saucy teenage girls, but he went on, bragging about the big bag of weed he was carrying. Immediately, my scheming mind clicked into gear, and I thought of the business opportunity that bag of pot represented. We were broke and the chance seemed too good to pass up. When our driver stopped for gas and to hit the men's room, I quickly sketched out my plan to Rhonda.

We grabbed the whole bag of pot, jumped out of the car, and hid, stifling our laughter and praying that he wouldn't find us. After he came out of the restroom and searched around, he finally gave up. In a frustrated exit, he and his car roared off into the winter night. That left us to continue on foot through the freezing Iowa cold until at last we arrived at Rhonda's mother's house.

To our chagrin, after all that time and travel, no one was home. We'd never thought of that possibility! Our hearts sank, but our enterprising minds clicked into gear again. Cold and desperate, we started checking the doors on nearby houses and eventually found an unlocked house across the street. We went right ahead and helped ourselves to the true necessities: a blanket, pillows and, of course, beer. Then we snuck out as quickly as we could, our hearts pounding, until we were sure that we'd gotten away undetected.

We found an open pickup truck parked on the street and climbed in to lie low and wait for Rhonda's mother to return. As it turned out, one single blanket didn't do much to protect two skinny girls from the piercing Iowa cold and wind. For warmth, we held each other tight and still shivered, teeth chattering. Time seemed to slow to a crawl and then stop altogether. After what seemed like an eternity, Rhonda's mother finally came home, and we showed up on her doorstep. She was startled to say the least, but she let us come in and we were finally in warmth and shelter. Both she and Rhonda were overjoyed to finally meet one another as were her half-sisters and stepfather.

The next day it dawned on me to call my mother, who I was sure had been agonizing over my disappearance. When she heard the whole story any worry quickly turned to anger. Now of course, as a parent myself, I can completely understand her sickening fear and her anger at my thoughtless and risky "adventure." But at the time I was taken aback and hadn't really thought through how she would react. Her message was firm.

"After what you've put me through, I don't want to see your face around here again. You chose to go away. Now stay away!"

Rhonda got a similar response when she called her great-aunt. We decided the ultimatums suited us just fine. We'd stay with Rhonda's mother and sell the marijuana to fund our spending money. We did this for the next two months. We bonded quickly with Rhonda's half-sisters, enrolled in school, made friends and enjoyed our "new family." Rhonda and her mother, although separated for all those years, formed a quick and loving bond.

That said, two girls, new to town, going around and selling pot had its risks. Eventually we were busted. Rhonda and I were packed off to jail in a neighboring town. I will never forget the officer's pride in hanging our "bag-of-gold" pot in the display case with all their other illegal finds. The next morning we traveled to Illinois in the back of a police car. The juvenile detention center in Rockford was our next stop. Once there we were put in isolation for our own protection, mostly because of the rougher girls already in custody. The officers were wise to protect us. Rhonda's family got her out after one night, but I was left alone and the long hours turned into days. To teach me a lesson, my mother left me there for three agonizing days. When I finally got out, she made it absolutely clear that I had better play by the rules and shape up or ship out. Overall, I'm thankful for my mother's tough love; it taught me a great deal.

Back in Illinois I was broke and on major homebound "probation" with my mother. But once again, I moved forward, picked myself up, and landed a job. I rented a room in the basement of a house owned by an elderly woman. The place was within walking distance of my new job. I continued to contribute every penny I could to help my mother, who continued to raise Audra and Mark on her own. I also continued to find my fair share of trouble. I easily entered the world of partying, made all the wrong types of friends, and lost what innocence I had left in those wild days.

A year passed. My mother was working for a man who owned several manufacturing companies, and the two decided that if I spent some time doing factory work, I might be motivated to develop bigger goals for my life. Perhaps an experience like factory work would force me to grow up and be more mature. I began work in a lawnmower factory that was an hour away. My mother's boss even helped to acquire an old car for me, so I could make that long drive.

It was definitely a learning experience. I worked alongside some incredibly tough women. The work was dirty and dangerous, and I remember that my hands were always cut up. You had to be fully alert, every second of every shift. This wasn't just because of the dangers of the job, but also the dangers of simply walking to your car, fearing the wrath of a tough coworker.

I also lived in constant dread that the other women would find out that I knew the owner. I was afraid they'd think that I had pulled some strings and taken a job away from someone else, or worse, that I was a mole. Even though I had to earn my own way in life from now on, I was afraid they'd regard me as a privileged kid playing on her mom's relationship with the owner. I was determined to work as hard as I could and show that I was doing just as good a job as anyone else in that factory. And despite the dangerous painful work, it was the best money I'd ever made. With the extra money, I could really make a difference and help my mom. I kept my head down and focused on doing the best I could, each and every day. I now had the responsibilities of paying rent, getting myself to work, keeping food on my table; and although I may have been on my own, my dedication to my family never ceased.

My evenings were often lonely. After my mother made the decision to kick me out of the house, she was determined to keep me apart from my sister. This filled me with a throbbing ache, a sense of emptiness that I could never seem to fill. I had basically raised Audra from when she was a baby and I felt like she was my own child. I often cried in my bed at night until I finally fell asleep from exhaustion. Months dragged by before my mother would let me see Audra again, very slow painful months. Audra had been the only thing in my life I had really loved, and to be kept from her seemed to me more painful than anything else I had experienced in my life.

In all of this, I was growing up and gaining independence, experiencing the highs and lows that come with being on your own. I may have missed some of the years that other kids spend learning in the classroom, but I was getting an education in the ways of the world.

Dreams

One day I decided I had had enough, I thought back to the days when I cleaned coffee pots and how I longed to have a desk that bore my name. I opened the local newspaper and gleaned the columns for jobs. With nothing more than an eighth grade education and a plethora of odd jobs, I figured, what do I have to lose and why don't I at least try? I needed to make a living and in my bold and brash way, I applied for a sales job with a high-end printing company. I had not one of the skills they were seeking, yet I landed that job, which included a company car and a sweet benefits package. I was soon immersed into the world of fine printing papers and offset printing and yes, I had my own desk with my name on it. Within weeks I was sent to Kenosha, Wisconsin to spend a week undergoing training at a paper plant. It was more than an out-of-body experience for a woman in her late teens. My fellow attendees had been in the business for years, yet they gracefully accepted me and were eager to help me along in my profession. My newfound success meant that I could rent a lovely apartment and treat my brother and sister to outings we had never experienced in the past. It also made me attractive, on more than one level to the opposite sex, something I was soon to find out.

Mother's birthday at her office

Mother, Mark, Audra, and me — going it alone

My brother Mark

My cousin, Keena Rothhammer

My training in Kenosha, WI (back row)

My brother Mark with his sons, Michael and Mark

CHAPTER FOUR

La Madre

Mother earth, I feel your history

Father sun, with you I have warmth

Sister rain, bring me the sustenance of life

Brother wind, speak to my spirit

Love, prayer, need, hunger...life

My soul seeks all that is powerful, holy and real

Take me to the four corners of the earth and allow me life after life until the end and beyond

With each life, I love, I struggle, toil and learn

All you have for me is all that I have for you

Each time, the lessons learned carry me to you

Another shot at this. What did I learn? Did I flourish? How did I survive?

Did I hate? Was I cruel? Did I sleep with peace or lie with the devil?

Did you see me there in the woods, the smell of musk heavy on my thighs

The look of fear or the sedation of love?

I was there, you see, lying, oh so quiet among the mist

It's no secret, I've always been a work-hard, play-hard gal, especially in my late teens and early twenties. While I'd been juggling adult responsibilities since I was twelve, I also had the typical adolescent desire to party, socialize, and cut loose. I probably did more than my fair share of socializing—I had so much time to make up for!

I had been such a social outcast as a young child, and from age twelve I was focused so fiercely on sheer survival for Mark, Audra, and myself, that there was precious little time for social pleasures. Although I was working every chance I got, taking as many hours as I could get wherever possible, I had a young person's energy and made time to play and party until all hours.

When I was twenty-two, I dated a nice guy, David Buckler, and we enjoyed our share of good times. Our affection grew and we both were tuned into a natural sexual attraction. I viewed myself as savvy about the ways of the world, and I made sure we took all the proper precautions. I was an independent, liberated woman, and I wanted to keep control over my body and my future. When my period was late, I turned every possibility over in my mind, trying to avoid the obvious conclusion. I ran all the excuses through my head: I must be worn out, I might be counting wrong, maybe I had just skipped a period for some reason. Yet as the days ticked past, the answer was inevitable: I must be pregnant.

I finally made an appointment at a clinic to schedule a pregnancy test. When I saw the result—a clear and unambiguous "positive," my first thought was the financial burden that lay ahead. I'd only begun to earn enough money to keep body and soul together. For the first time, I'd also broken loose from feeling parental responsibilities toward Mark and Audra. I was finally enjoying some personal freedom and independence. In months, I'd be completely responsible for another human being, an infant.

I was awestruck that a new life was growing inside me, that I would nurture a soul who would find its way into the world, and at the possibility of giving that person the very best life I could. I was terrified that my boyfriend, my mother, my friends, my boss would reject me and leave me alone and outcast, just as I'd found a foothold in the big, cold world. That said, I was already fiercely attached to this new person, whoever he or she was, and determined to fight, making the best of it for us both.

Marriage and Motherhood

David was the kind of upstanding person who would, as we said in those days, "do the right thing." We got married, and when I was twenty-three my first son, Justin, came into this world. I was overcome with so many new and powerful feelings. It was like being overtaken by wave after wave in a turbulent ocean; every time I thought I'd caught my breath and found some balance, I'd be washed over again. I felt such tenderness for this infant, for this new person entering the world with complete innocence and trust. I was in love, truly in love with Justin. Never before had I felt love on this level and my life would never be the same.

But, given my own fraught history, I was also terrified. I truly did not know what remnants from my history as a victim of abuse might surface, affecting my own behavior. Deep down, I feared I would hurt him or abuse him. In my childhood, parents hurt their children and that was all I knew. Here was this precious bundle I loved, but deep in my soul was a searing terror that I would be the agent of pain. Sometimes I even tied myself to the bed at night, afraid that without restraints I might roam about in some state of unknown mental capacity—just as I had talked in my sleep as a foster kid. I was frightened that I would do the things I rejected with all my heart but knew to be a possibility. I understood everything an adult could do to a defenseless child, even an infant.

The stress of living with these horrifying mental scenarios, coupled with my own ever-present past and the tender ache of new motherhood, was a nightmare. The fear I had of hurting my son was constant and incredibly disturbing. I couldn't get the alarming possibilities out of my mind, though I recoiled with disgust whenever I thought of what might happen. My emotions would swing high and low, from love to terror, and at times I thought I couldn't bear it a moment longer. Yet, somehow, I overcame it all and became a loving and protective mother.

I always gave my children a home with unconditional love. I took up golfing and skiing, so they might enjoy those sports also. I made the commitment early in their lives that they would receive the best education, live comfortably and that travel would be a big part of their lives. I did churn through relationships because of my inability to trust or truly believe that I was worthy of another's heartfelt commitment and that had an effect on their lives that I regret. But I kept my intentions absolutely clear on one front: No matter where home might be, it was a safe and loving place. I worked especially hard at providing every advantage to my children: good schools, nice clothing and extraordinary vacations. I was determined that my children would never know the specters of my childhood, hunger, isolation or poverty. My path to privilege was not an easy one; I had to prove to my employers I could work harder, longer, and smarter than my counterparts. It was with this determination that I became a successful and respected businesswoman, which in turn, allowed me the opportunity to provide all those things to my children I had been denied in my own childhood.

Two years after Justin was born, my son Jarred was born. As with Justin, I found myself in love all over again. He was angelic, and it touched my heart to see the love his older brother had for him, as did his father. David was a loving and dedicated father, yet I found my old demons creeping in. My growing inability to love him put a strain on the marriage. This, coupled with my strong need to be independent, to be the breadwinner, was tanking my marriage. I felt as if I was sitting back watching a sad and out-of-control movie and there was not one damn thing I could do. I was helpless and heartbroken. To be honest, being home with two little ones and being completely financially dependent on someone else felt oppressive. My husband had no way of knowing or understanding why his solid efforts to support a growing family and give us a decent life left me feeling vulnerable and unfulfilled.

When the boys were three and one, I left him. It was a decision that tore my heart out and threw it to the floor and even to this day I can feel the pain of that moment. I knew the decision was my own and I didn't ask for or take anything that he had built up for us in the four years we were married. I wanted the boys' home to remain intact. I know what it feels like to have a parent leave you and take all you know. I also didn't feel that my husband, David, deserved to lose his wife and all his possessions. That didn't seem fair to me. He was confused and hurt, but in the end, he accepted my decision, if not my reasoning. We focused on doing what was best for the boys. Yet, for years, he waited for me, attempting to reconcile and provide a home for the boys with both mother and father. It was heart-wrenching to say "no" to him, time and time again, knowing that all he wanted was his family and that he truly loved me. I had no way of telling him that I was simply "broken" and would be for some time.

Co-Parenting and Career-Building

We amicably agreed on joint custody, and I willingly allowed the boys to mostly stay with David. He was their primary caregiver. This was frowned on at the time, and everyone from the people closest to me to casual work acquaintances openly disapproved. But I've never been afraid to stand up for what I thought was right, and I stuck to my guns no matter how many judgmental comments were directed at me. First and foremost, David deserved to be with the boys. He did not ask to separate, nor had he wanted to break apart our family. I also held the strong belief that the boys needed the powerful, positive influence of their father in their daily lives rather than growing up primarily in a woman's world. I also knew that I had the earning capacity to make a difference in my sons' lives, offering them the best schools, clothing and adventures. I wanted my sons to have it all regardless of the number of hours it took me to produce the income needed to afford what "all" is.

Although I'd given a lot of thought to my decisions, I did what I thought was best for my boys, putting my own feelings aside. Still, it was deeply painful for me. I spent my fair share of nights screaming out in pain and soaking my pillow with tears. Surrounded by so much disapproval about my life choices, I questioned my own decision at times. Many thought that I had abandoned my sons, and I was shamed and shunned. Joint custody was the best decision; David was a good father and the boys certainly wanted him in their lives. To this day I am proud that my children never heard me speak a bad word about their father and the bottom line is, I respected him. I believe that children need to hear loving and positive things about their parents from everyone, regardless of the situation.

Meanwhile, I focused on creating a career and worked to find a way to make a living—a good living. I was hungry for success, and I was as determined as a mother bear to give my boys everything possible. I pursued my real estate agent's license and worked incredibly hard to pass the licensing requirements. I remember the fear I felt when I completed the test in twenty minutes, especially since test-takers were allotted three hours. I was certain I had failed, missed something, or simply blanked out from the stress. I waited three agonizing weeks for my test results to arrive, and I was in complete disbelief at my high scores.

Then, with determination and grit, I did the one extra thing that set me apart from others in the industry. My managing broker offered no interim pay or training period, so I accepted straight commission which meant it would be awhile before I'd see a check in my hand. Hard work was one thing I knew well, and I've never been afraid of it. This was the 1980s, the era of stagflation and sky-high interest rates. Real estate agents were dropping like flies as cautious consumers deferred making a home purchase that would lock them to a high interest rate loan for fifteen, twenty, or thirty years. I could not have chosen a worse profession.

In those days, real estate agents had to take care of all aspects of a deal, not just showing a client around and helping them negotiate the purchase price. I had to roll up my sleeves and line up financing, title work, and orchestrate every phase of the purchase process. I worked very hard to manage every detail and give my clients a level of attention that no one else would provide. I was the first person in the office and the last to leave, seven days a week. As the years went by, I built my base of residential real estate clients and earned their loyalty by making their every buying and selling experience the very best it could be.

As my reputation grew, I won industry awards and prospered financially. After all those years of grinding poverty and social rejection, and with little in the way of formal education, it was an amazing affirmation of my own capabilities. It was proof that I could make it on my own merit. Soon I was not only providing comfortably for our little family, but by the third year I was making six figures—a remarkable feat for a woman in this time period.

All this in addition to co-parenting and being single mom with two small children. My real estate career also afforded me the opportunity to spoil my baby sister, Audra, and I was awash in joy at all I could provide her. I was acutely aware that I must present an impeccably professional image in what is, after all, a very image-conscious business. I dressed well, kept my scars hidden, focused on expanding my vocabulary and grammar skills. And I never, ever hinted at the dark times in my past. I never let it slip that I had only finished eighth grade, or that I had suffered physical, sexual, and emotional abuse. And during this time in my career, I never mentioned my burns. I became someone else, someone the world would accept, although, I always remained mother and sister.

By then I was dating a very astute businessman, Phil Robinson, who had introduced the ten-minute oil change concept. Gradually I began to help him locate and secure business sites to develop his franchise and company-owned sites. Phil and I were kindred spirits, both from tough childhoods with an equal share of veracious business sense. I was hungry to learn all I could and Phil was a great teacher. Through this, I discovered that I had a knack for commercial real estate, and I made the transition to that department in the real estate company.

I went on to negotiate business deals at a whole different level with huge organizations like Quaker State and Lube Pros. My commercial commission checks had some extra zeros over those from my residential work, and I was thrilled at all the new opportunities in my future. At the time, the commercial department was an all-male bastion, and I was excluded from the boozy, clubby world that my male peers inhabited. But I focused on the work and didn't let myself get distracted by the subtle exclusions and petty put-downs that I experienced daily from my male colleagues.

Phil and I worked closely to develop his commercial sites that included oil-change centers. That experience led me to develop other commercial sites, including strip malls and car washes. I tracked down coveted corner lots for redevelopment. Nearly all of the lots were once gas stations with tanks that had leaked. At the time, the EPA standards for clean sites (called Level 1) had just come out, which meant that the sites would have to be dug up and all the contaminated dirt and other materials needed to be hauled away before redevelopment could start. This was a stressful and highly detailed commitment, and not many commercial real estate agents had the stomach to take on these projects. Every time I hoped against hope that each load excavated would test clean. This was rarely the case, there was more work to do—which meant the deal couldn't close and I would not receive commission checks as quickly as I'd hoped.

I persevered, rolled up my sleeves, and spent as much time as I needed on-site, making sure that the former gas station lots were brought up to comply with government standards, passing inspection. I built a reputation for being ethical, hardworking, and thorough. And my career blossomed. Eventually my dating relationship with Phil ended but we remained close friends. In fact, many years later, Phil was my birthing coach during my pregnancy with my daughter. The valuable experience of transitioning into the commercial side of the business continued to inspire me to grow and succeed and I will always be grateful to Phil for all he did.

After eight years in the real estate business, I grew restless. I was too independent-minded to think that I would ever enter into another long-term relationship. In fact, my Volvo sported custom plates that read "LUVPRUF." I wore my independence and self-sufficiency like a badge— or like armor to protect from ever feeling vulnerable or being hurt again.

In 1991, I charted a new course. I left the boys with their father, hopped in that Volvo with my dog, my golf clubs, and a few clothes, and took off on a whim for Charleston, South Carolina. The trip was very spontaneous. I told my assistant I'd be taking off for a while and had no idea of when I'd return. I wanted a change of scene, some time alone with my own thoughts, a few rounds of golf near the beach, and some space to breathe that was far from the pressures of work and the responsibilities of co-parenting the boys.

A Girl Walks into a Bar...

I made plans to dine out in Charleston with my girlfriend who lived there and some of her friends. We had to wait for a table at the restaurant, so we decided to grab a cocktail in the bar. A very handsome gentleman introduced himself as Greg and asked me what time it was. I thought very little of it at that moment, but when we finished dinner and dropped back by the bar area, there was Greg, smiling directly at me. We all ended up chatting and the conversation flowed naturally and easily. To my surprise, I noticed he was wearing a watch that kept perfect time. Soon we were headed downtown to a great high-energy nightclub.

Although he was a large, well-built man, Greg was amazing agile on the dance floor. I was so impressed with his grace and his moves; he was truly in tune with the music at every moment. By the end of the evening we had migrated to a small jazz club—and I was growing more interested in him. We spent several hours seated at the bar enjoying easy conversation. He had such confidence, a warm tone to his voice, and the slightest hint of vulnerability. I was entranced, and I gave him my phone number. The very next day he called to invite me to spend the day at his beach condo.

As the day at his beach house unfolded, I felt as if I had entered some magical land or an enchanting dream, one wonderful moment leading to the next, and the next and the next. The long romantic afternoon naturally unfolded into an even more romantic night together. Ultimately, we spent an entire week together, playing in the surf and sharing our innermost thoughts and dreams. We both knew it was just an interlude with no expectations of each other for the future.

Away from the pressures of our everyday lives, we dropped deeply and freely into a zone of trust, confidence, and pleasure. I felt that nothing in my life before or after could be any better than those precious days. Surprisingly, I was able to let down some of the walls I typically put up with men and allowed Greg a glimpse into the real me. When I later discovered I was pregnant, I knew this child would be special, and that one day he or she would want to know how they'd come to be. It turned out the child was a girl. She was not a "mistake," she was a God-given gift.

Going it Alone

I waited several weeks before telling Greg that I was expecting. He suggested that I terminate the pregnancy. Understandably, he had other priorities in his life, and we'd known from the start that we couldn't be together for the long term. As I considered my options, I grew determined to have this baby on my own and raise the child myself. Since my divorce from David, I had been co-parenting the boys well, even though they had an involved and committed father. I had a thriving career and a survivor's resourcefulness. I was fully confident that I could rise to the challenge of mothering this child, standing on my own two feet. I not only accepted the challenge, I embraced it.

I was not prepared for my mother's reaction when I told her my plan. I'd never seen her in such a cold fury. In a way, it was more frightening than when she had chased after me with the metal vacuum cleaner attachment. She agreed with Greg that I should terminate the pregnancy. She feared I would jeopardize my career, or worse, lose it all together. She made a valid point of how a single woman with a straight commission job could go it alone, when in the past I'd had such difficult pregnancies. In the end, she never listened to any of my reasons for wanting to raise this child. In that moment, I was her child and she was terrified for me and my future.

Just months before I met Greg, I had undergone my third surgery for endometriosis. After the surgery, my doctor told me that I should not expect to have any more children. His opinion was that the repeated surgeries and scarring had rendered me barren. I could not have been more overjoyed than when I discovered I was pregnant. Naively, I thought everyone else would be thrilled as well.

I was completely baffled by my mother's strong reaction. She was raised Catholic, and I could not comprehend her desire for me to terminate the pregnancy. At the time, I asked myself why her reaction was so emotional. Years later, I learned why. It turned out that when she was just out of high school, she had gotten pregnant. For a German Catholic family, there was no greater disgrace. Her parents sent her away from their farm in Wisconsin to a Catholic facility for unwed mothers in Arkansas. At the facility, her family's hometown neighbors wouldn't see her swelling belly, and she wouldn't be fodder for the town's gossip and sharp tongues. She simply did not want me to experience the same pain.

She delivered the baby, a little girl, when she was just nineteen—alone and far away from the support of her family. The baby was immediately taken from her to give to adoptive parents. My mother had never been able to speak about this to anyone back home, even with family members. The shameful episode had weighed on her for years, a festering dark secret. After I learned this, I understood why my mother's reaction had been so extreme, and why she was so adamant that I terminate my own pregnancy. It broke my heart to think of all those long years that she lived with that heartbreaking secret.

But I stayed true to myself, and I made the conscious decision to have Hillary and raise her alone, without disrupting her father's life. All I had to mark my time with Greg was a few photos, a shirt of his and, as the years unfolded, an occasional note. I also kept a journal throughout my pregnancy, eager to document every aspect of this life-changing time. I kept all these things in a shoebox that I carefully guarded through every move and transition in the decades that followed. That box became a special part of my world wherever I went, and I treated it with tender and loving care. I would often spend time reading my pregnancy journal, looking at the few photos of Greg, and his carefully folded shirt, remembering our time together with hopeless longing. I wanted Hillary to understand that her life rose out of a time of incredible joy, when my heart was bursting with happiness and the night stars presented an endless canopy of beauty and wonder. The sea and the surf were the soundtrack to our idyll, and I know, and I want Hillary to know, that she was absolutely meant to be.

I had originally planned to name the baby Charleston, to pay homage to that special time with her father and the city in which we met. But in the end I decided I did not want to burden her with such a literal reminder, and I named her Hillary instead. I regret that decision; she reflects the name in both looks and deeds, she seems to me most certainly to be "Charlie."

My plans of raising this child on my own with the assistance of a nanny were not going as I'd hoped they would. In those days, nanny services were few and those I interviewed didn't seem to offer the care and background checks I sought for my unborn child. I became frantic and then agitated, but then had an idea. I would open my own agency and through this process not only did I find a nanny for Hillary, I developed a lucrative business that added to my real estate earnings and provided a much-needed service to the community.

In the first twenty-five years of her life, Hillary only saw her father seven times, but I continued to speak of him lovingly and kept a photo of him in a heart shaped frame next to her bed. He was primarily focused on his career, his new wife and raising her two sons. It was not easy raising her alone. The financial burden was one thing, but the real killer was the emotional stress. How do you explain to a toddler that she has no father? When the other children at school have one. On occasion, Greg would send Christmas gifts or a card which further confused Hillary and his infrequent visits were awkward at best. As time went on, he was hit by a series of terrible misfortunes and lost his job, his entire savings, his health—and yes, his wife. He required hospice care and Hillary began to travel to Florida to help care for him as his health declined.

It was a tough way to get to know her father, especially when she had felt rejected by him for so long. But in the end, we were all grateful that Hillary and her father had the chance to get to know one another more deeply. I had no illusions that they might one day become close, although that would have been nice. Considering Hillary grew up in a single parent household, she turned out remarkably well. She is a kind, thoughtful and incredibly intuitive young woman. As with all my children, I am proud and humbled to be a part of her life.

Over the years, I did my best to make sure that Hillary's father knew how much I treasured our brief time together, and that I have never regretted those days in the sun. Despite the fact that we didn't raise Hillary together, I held no malice toward him on any level, which I deeply hope he fully understood. The result of our time together was a precious gift beyond all words: my beloved daughter, my precious Hillary.

David and me

An unexpected visit from my father, following the birth of my second child, Jarred

Precious time spent with my son, Jarred

The boys and me, 1991

Real estate days with my "Luvpruf" Volvo

With Justin at his kindergarten graduation

Audra and me with Jarred

My sister, Audra, Justin and Jarred

Golf tournament with Jarred

Jarred and me on the slopes

Jarred and Hillary

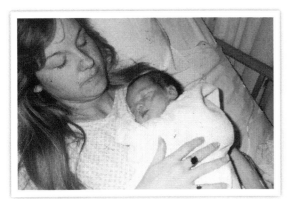

The moment I met Hillary

Hillary's father, Greg Swindell

Hillary, one beautiful gift

Photo shoot for my nanny service

Hillary, one happy child

Ski trip to Colorado with Hillary, 1997

The children and me at Hilton Head Island

CHAPTER FIVE

Angels are No Strangers to Chains

Carry me forward, carry me high
Let me feel the sun that hangs above the bright, blue sky
Forever now, forever then, forever me
But can't you see I was back, ready to try again
My sins were listed and my back broke
I played in the flames and savored my own smoke
You came to me with a whisper and I came to you with my sword
You offered grace and understanding, I found none
I'll be with you there, forever and after, my love

A Lonely Path

Although my real estate career continued to prosper, it was difficult, to say the least. As a single woman who'd decided to have a baby on her own in a conservative town, I stayed focused on my career and was a top-producing real estate agent in our well-regarded firm. My life was lonely, yet fulfilling. Every waking moment was spent either working long hours or with my three children.

Despite my career success, my status as a single working mother caused my co-workers to treat me with disdain and, at times, flat-out resentment.

They waited for me to fail and when I didn't, it only seemed to raise their level of disgust. The situation grew worse when the local, glossy *Rockford Magazine* contacted me because they wanted to do a feature story. The angle for the piece was "Rockford's Own Murphy Brown"—based on a then popular television show that also featured a single mother. The owner of my real estate firm was a longtime, significant advertiser with the magazine. When he got wind of the project he called me into his office and made it clear that there would be no such story. A pregnant single woman was not something he or his firm was proud of or wanted to advertise.

Beyond my own office, I faced rejection and a cold shoulder everywhere I went in town. Even my own mother was against me having a child as a single parent. As the pregnancy progressed, a new strength rose up inside me. There was much more going on than my growing midsection. I was doing what so many women before me had to do in secret and I was proud. I fought my way forward, knowing that the path I was blazing would benefit other women in the future.

My pregnancies were always difficult and like my first two, I spent much time in the hospital, hooked up to IVs, and praying for relief. I suffered from constant nausea and vomiting the entire nine months. This was before our medical community understood and could diagnose the debilitating effects of hyperemesis gravidarum, a condition that takes morning sickness to a whole new level. The condition produces, all day and all night, nine months of misery. Despite this additional obstacle, I stuck to my guns about my choice. I managed to hide my illness and all the while continued to be a top-producing agent. Given that Rockford's a fairly large city—in fact, the largest city in Illinois outside of Chicago— you would expect that it might be rather progressive. But it's not. It's a very conservative, insular place.

Despite my struggles and isolation, I have absolutely no regrets. The social and community slights I suffered are nothing in comparison to the joy and beauty Hillary has brought to my life, year after year. In fact, the hate and disdain shown me only proved to make me stronger.

And I never lost my focus. Just three days after she was born, I was back at work. It was a matter of necessity since it was a commission-only job. Now, in addition to contributing to the support of my two sons, I also had the new expense of caring for another child, including a nanny to stay with her while I was at work. I am grateful to this day for the kind and courageous support that my ex-husband, David, and his new wife, Peggy, showed me. They were, in fact, the only two people who supported my decision to have Hillary. They became second parents to my daughter, a wonderful addition to both her life and theirs.

Change of Heart, Change of Career

When Hillary was less than a year old, I was helping a client, Jim, with a closing for a strip mall center he had purchased. In the course of our conversation, he mentioned a small company he had recently bought, VanHolten's, the inventor of the Pickle-in-a-Pouch. The more we talked, the more intrigued I grew. This sounded like a company with potential, an opportunity that just needed some vision and drive to make it succeed.

Soon I began dating Jim, and I had a chance to look at VanHolten's more closely. I became more convinced that this was a true turnaround challenge. I never shy away from a difficult project, and I had developed a broad range of formidable business skills. Before long, I decided to give up my lucrative real estate career and turn my full attention to VanHolten's.

VanHolten's was a fourth-generation family-owned company in Wisconsin, more than one hundred years old. They began as a vinegar manufacturer, and then moved into sauerkraut and pickles. Despite its innovative introduction of the Pickle-in-a-Pouch, the company had been long neglected and was falling apart. By the time my client bought it,

VanHolten's was nearly run into the ground. The phones rang constantly, but the calls were from bill collectors, not prospective customers.

Despite the fact that my romance with the owner came to an end, I continued to be deeply involved and committed to my work at VanHolten's, and we maintained a productive and healthy working relationship. In my typical all-or-nothing fashion, I was soon involved in every aspect of the company. They had never seriously thought about the marketing and branding side of the business, so in addition to the financial turnaround focus, I also built out the national broker network and developed some fun new pickles products: Hot Mama, Big Papa and Little Pepe. Before the new products were on the market, we were incurring too much waste by limiting our sizes and flavors. The development of these new products reduced waste and increased profits. Pickles in a pouch were fine as far as they went, but we also needed a "hook."

I had a lot of fun working with the graphic designers, particularly as we worked on branding Little Pepe. I kept in mind our significant and growing customer base in the southern U.S. and their zest for all things HOT. With this particular pickle, we turned up the heat with the addition of more capsicum, an ingredient that adds to the fiery flavor. We had a lot of fun developing the graphics. Hot Mama and Big Pappa allowed us to use the larger pickles in production and reduce waste.

I was very fortunate that my boss was so supportive of my initiative and gave me a lot of creative freedom and support. Today VanHolten's is still run by his son, Steve Byrnes. It's been so rewarding seeing how they have continued to grow and prosper, and they still market the pickles I helped create all those years ago. I'm proud of how far they've come and I love walking into a store and seeing their products.

But the job was demanding and I was constantly on the road. Hillary and my nanny frequently traveled with me. This way I could maintain close ties to my daughter while still giving everything I could to a job that

I loved. The travel was constant, sometimes for three weeks straight. I'd often stay in one city during weekends, rather than fly home and back to another location. This saved the company money and allowed me a bit of rest. It was great to have Hillary by my side, although it was a tough juggling single motherhood with a career. I was a young woman in a man's world. That said, I never interpreted it that way. All I saw were my goals, both for the company and for my family. Ultimately, we pulled the company from the brink of bankruptcy and set it on a path to solid business success.

In my second year, Jim allowed me to hire an assistant. Cindy was not only intelligent and hard-working, she was fun-loving. I set her up in my office, since I needed her to be a clone of me and know all aspects of the business. I also took her with me to trade shows and on outings where we would work and entertain our brokers. Cindy and I became very close and it was a joy to work with her. Until this time in my adult life, I'd never felt quite so close to another woman. We worked endless hours and made some great headway for the company and, of course, we played hard every chance we got.

At one point, we invited all the brokers from across the country to Minneapolis for training and team-building. Cindy and I took them out for a fun evening at a gay club that had the best dancing in the area. Amid the merriment and the adult beverages, I found myself enjoying a dance with one of my Texas brokers, and out of the blue, he grabbed me and kissed me full on, in view of everyone. I was at first shocked, then quite intrigued. His name was Greg, although I would eventually call him by his middle name, Haydn. As the evening progressed, and against my own rules, we found ourselves in a more romantic kiss—and it was the most amazing kiss of my life. It was just the beginning of an incredible, passionate, and whirlwind relationship. One that would nearly kill me.

Gone to Texas

People tried to warn me about my dating Haydn, but I didn't listen and didn't care. I was in love. He'd swept me off my feet. In just a few short months, I found myself in New York City, getting married in the cathedral of St. John the Divine. It was amazing to stand at the altar, next to a statue of Joan of Arc with one of the blocks from her prison cell at my feet. Our wedding night was spent at the Met, enjoying the incredible opera, *La Bohème*. At the time, it was a fairy tale and I was living every moment of it. Hillary and I gave up our beloved home in Wisconsin and moved to San Antonio, Texas. I helped Haydn take over the payments on the home he had shared with his ex-wife, suitable for our newly blended family. I brought my furnishings, art and decor to ensure the home felt comfortable and welcoming for us. But as the relationship progressed, I was puzzled by some of Haydn's behaviors. Some days he would come home warm, loving, and happy. Yet on other days, he seemed down and distant, and I couldn't understand the reason for these strange disconnects. On the whole we were very happy, or so it seemed.

I continued to travel for business. During a planned business trip to Los Angeles, I extended my stay, taking some vacation days with the plan of flying Haydn out for a few special days together. I was excited and happy as I put the finishing touches on our upcoming rendezvous, which I had planned as a treat for Haydn's birthday. He had never been to that part of the country and I was excited to show him my favorite spots from Monterey to San Francisco. Anticipating the trip, I called him to lock in some details and discuss our romantic getaway. That's when he told me he wanted a divorce, further confusing me by saying that he was still willing to come to California for our trip. I will never forget the hotel bed I sat on, the color of the walls, the feel of the phone in my hand, and the pain in my heart.

I was completely shocked; I felt like I'd been hit in the face with a large rock. I canceled the California plans and arranged to catch the next flight home. I didn't know what was happening or where to turn. I reached out to my friends, crying, unable to make sense of it. It took four flights to make it home and thankfully this was back in the day when planes had phones. I would settle away from everyone, alone in the back, sobbing and make call after call, trying to make sense of this destruction. While in route, I spoke to a neighbor who was also a friend. She asked why there were movers at my house. This made no sense. Haydn had owned nothing but a single mattress when I married him. Why would movers be at the house and where were they going with my belongings?

My neighbor was right. Haydn had the movers take all my possessions and my children's things, right down to the art on the walls, putting everything haphazardly in storage. Haydn picked me up at the airport, in my Volvo, and drove me by the storage unit, allowing me to view all I owned and my precious memories in a disheveled mess.

Devastated and heartbroken, I threw the one suitcase I had and my Bible in the car and drove nonstop from San Antonio all the way back to Madison, Wisconsin. Fortunately, Hillary—age four—had been visiting my ex-husband and his wife, so she didn't have to witness my devastation or deal with the abrupt change and uncertainty. I was free to completely focus on trying to piece our lives back together and get us past this dark place.

With no place of my own to stay, I bunked with Cindy and borrowed my boss's credit card to buy clothes. I was due at a trade show in Washington D.C., the following week, and I needed to look professional. Even in my emotionally shattered state, I knew I had to stay focused on my job. Both Jim and Cindy were tremendously supportive and literally provided the glue that held me together. I slept with my Bible held to my breast every night, crying myself to sleep, and praying I could hold on and survive.

I managed to get through that trade show, and I painfully, slowly, tried to pick up the pieces of my life. I spent the next few weeks in a daze, sleepwalking through the daily demands of career and motherhood while trying to understand what had happened. Had I misjudged things so badly, not realizing Haydn never truly loved me? Had I done or said something that triggered this abrupt and total rejection? Everything seemed fine when I set off for the trip to L.A. What could have changed?

As I groped my way forward, others who'd known Hayden longer than I did gave me a glimpse of sides of him I'd never suspected. I learned that he had a history of recklessness in relationships and had been an unreliable partner and friend to others before me. The mood swings I'd found so baffling resulted from his struggles with substance abuse—his addiction to speed. This was something he'd so carefully and successfully hidden from me. I was so naïve, I didn't possess the ability to identify a drug user. Much later, Haydn told me that he'd divorced me in order to protect me from the issues that arose from his addiction. But at the time I knew only pain and confusion.

I had no idea where we would live, even what city or state. I finally worked up the energy and courage to return to San Antonio and retrieve my belongings from the storage unit. Then I completed divorce proceedings. Haydn turned on the charm and tried to talk me into coming back. Like the beginning of our courtship, he chose to be passionate and devoted. The memories of our many happy times together called to me like a Siren. But in the end, there was no way for me to get past the pain he'd caused. I remained resolute, determined to never fall into a position again where I would be vulnerable or jeopardize the safety of my children.

I moved Haydn out of the house and sold it; I couldn't bear living in the place we had shared together, surrounded by memories of him, of us. By now, many of my clients were in the Southwest, and after giving it a great deal of thought, I decided to stay in San Antonio and make it our home. I bought a new place for Hillary and me and collected all my belongings from storage. I was starting over, a part of me was broken. I was fragile and frightened—yet that fighting spirit deep in my soul was once again calling my name.

Venue Change

I was determined to rebuild my life and move forward. Like previous experiences, I was hit hard with a devastating setback. So once again I squared my shoulders and faced the future with every ounce of courage I could muster. My thoughts frequently returned to a conversation I'd had with a psychiatrist in my late twenties. I've rarely had the luxury of time or resources to see a therapist. But during this one time period, I worked with an outstanding counselor and had developed a very deep level of trust with him, his judgment, and his intentions. Not an easy thing for me, especially then. One day, when I talked through some of the issues I struggled with, he stopped, looked me straight in the eye, and said, "You are remarkably intact."

I must have looked confused because he went on to say, "Most people who have suffered even a fraction of the abuse you've endured are either dead, are a substance abuser, or are in jail."

I was dumbstruck. I considered myself to be one of the least intact people on the planet. I was uplifted by his statement and his confidence, believing I had overcome obstacles that defeated other poor souls. Since he told me this, the therapist's words have always been a great inspiration to me. Throughout my life, therapists and friends have suggested I write a book. There was no way I would consent to having all my secrets and pain laid out for all to see. Yet, later in life, with the encouragement and support of a trusted Moonlight Fund board member and friend, Deborah Ortiz de la Peña, I decided to write this book to share my story and hopefully inspire others. I thought of the psychiatrist's words and I knew I had my title and yes, I am "remarkably intact."

In the meantime, back to my post-Haydn days. I focused on my friends, my career, and on Hillary. One thing I did to invest in myself and my career was to join a country club. This gave me the opportunity to stay physically fit at the gym, as well as to play golf with my growing roster of clients. I was exercising with a friend at the club one day when she discreetly pointed to a man named Dick Jones. My friend said that Dick was interested in getting to know me better. She added, "Not now. He went through a divorce last year, but he's interested in getting to know you in the future."

After that, over a period of many months, Dick and I began to cross paths at the club fairly regularly. One day when we were chatting, he handed me his business card and told me to call him later. During the few conversations we'd had at the club, I had found Dick to be intelligent, charismatic, and a very capable businessman. Since I was a focused career person too, I respected his professionalism and accomplishments, and I enjoyed getting to know that side of Dick. I also liked the way he talked and the way he walked.

Eventually, I called Dick's office. He was out of the office and his assistant answered. A part of me wanted to drop the line, I felt so out of my league, yet, when I mentioned my name, she immediately told me to hold on. The next thing I knew, my heart leapt as I was patched through to Dick's mobile line. He greeted me warmly, pleased that I had called. It was instantly clear to me that this was a man of genuine power and import. After a lovely conversation, I accepted his invitation to go to dinner. The entire experience reminded me of a scene out of the movie *9 ½ Weeks*.

Our date was a lovely evening, and the time flew by as we easily conversed about all kinds of topics. Dick was knowledgeable, interesting, and funny, and I felt more relaxed and attractive that evening than I had in a very long time. After dinner, he invited me back to his gorgeous showcase home, designed by the renowned Texas architect Dick Clark.

Entering his home that evening, I knew I was not good enough for this man of such great wealth and means. Yet there I was. In my typical spontaneous fashion, I disrobed and entered the hot tub, this certainly pleased Dick and he followed suit. As we kissed and explored one another's bodies, Dick said the most extraordinary thing, "I'm more interested in a second date than I am in conquering you tonight."

Our relationship blossomed and a year later we were engaged. Dick Jones was a highly respected and visible member of the San Antonio business and social community. In many ways, marrying him felt like an out-of-body experience. I had such tremendous respect and admiration for him, as did everyone in town. How could Celia, the little burned kid, be Dick Jones's wife, hobnobbing with the city's elite and with the celebrities whose circles he moved in? Yet here I was, watching myself as if in a dream as we traveled to exotic destinations, enjoying lazy days on the beach at St. Bart's, and going on shopping sprees at exclusive New York retailers.

Perhaps the greatest blessing of being Mrs. Jones was that I could now be a full-time mom and enroll my children in the best prep schools available. From the time they first began attending school, I made sure they attended the best schools I could afford. Now I was able to kick that up a few notches and provide them an education that most children only dream of. I was so grateful that Dick supported me in this effort and it gave me the greatest joy to see each of them flourish in this new, yet challenging environment. My eldest, Justin, had always been a bit shy, so I encouraged him to join the football team and my younger son, Jarred, joined the Corps of Cadets at TMI, while my daughter, Hillary, attended Keystone and continued her dance lessons. They were flourishing in their new worlds and I was so proud of their achievements.

Yet along with the glamor and freedom, I felt an enormous amount of pressure. Dick was relaxed and supportive, accepting me for exactly who I was, but I never felt like I comfortably filled the role of a country club wife. I felt like I didn't quite fit in, and that everyone around me felt it, too.

For example, I'd be dressed to the nines for a charity gala but would wear combat boots under my dress. I'd host lavish parties in our showcase home. At the same time, I was fully aware that the people standing in my living room, drinking cocktails, were gossiping about me when I was out of earshot. It felt like déjà vu all over again. After my childhood of being ostracized for being ugly and for being the weird burned kid, here I was an attractive, well-to-do woman married to a scion of San Antonio society. And I still felt rejection at every turn. It was a great strain to keep up with the expectations of someone in a highly visible position in the "society" world. I had to look like a million bucks, keep my figure slender and my body perfectly toned, and be the life of the party night after night.

Even though marrying Dick put me in social positions that pressed the buttons, reminding me of excruciating emotional childhood pain, it also was a time of great personal freedom, acceptance, and love from a wonderful husband. Dick encouraged all of my dreams and gifts. For the first time, I allowed myself to think about and possibly realize my dream of helping people. I allowed Dick to support me financially. This way I could fully devote myself to giving and building something with a greater purpose. It was a huge step for me to quit my job and rely on someone else to support me.

I loved and adored Dick, yet I lacked the ability to show him or to trust my emotions. This caused him great heartache and confusion. I was, by all accounts, still broken. Yet, all along, Dick continued to be my champion in all things, he took up skiing, accompanied me to burn-related fundraising events and stood by as I worked the countless hours necessary to put the Moonlight Fund into action. He took an interest in my children, accompanying me to football games, dance recitals, and military corps events. He also made one of my biggest dreams come true by enrolling them in the best prep schools in the area. On all accounts, Dick was a committed husband and a loving step father.

Living a dream and creating a dream are very different. One has to start somewhere, and in the beginning, this dream involved a lot of learning and self-reflection. At heart, I was a simple girl from a conservative, backward town, and all the social pretense surrounding the country club life was off-putting. And as I continued to look for ways to invest my time, now that I was not consumed with my career, I discovered I had a new and growing passion to help burn survivors. This is when I started to volunteer at the Brooke Army Medical Center in San Antonio. The beginning of my greater purpose in life began to sprout in my mind.

Dick remained loyal and loving as I engaged more deeply in my work with burn survivors, although I struggled with my role as a socialite. Over time, and with his gentle encouragement, I developed the courage for the first time in my life to wear short sleeves in public with the burn scars on my arm plainly visible for all to see. As my work and passion for supporting burn survivors grew, it seemed more and more hypocritical to cover up the reminders of my own experience. If part of my mission was to raise awareness of the needs of burn survivors, to encourage people to accept burn survivors fully into society and support them in rebuilding their lives, how could I justify acting as if I was ashamed of my scars?

It was not an easy transition, but I was determined. Those in high society really had something to talk about now! People couldn't keep themselves from staring—or worse—turning away when they saw me in short sleeves for the first time. Dick was supportive of what I was trying to accomplish, volunteering with burn survivors and their families. We also spoke at length about the lack of nonprofit support for burn survivors and their families. I had this novel idea of creating a nonprofit that actually conducted itself like a good old-fashioned charity. High giving, low overhead, and 24/7 support. Dick provided me with the seed money to get Moonlight Fund off the ground and enlisted his staff at Ernst & Young to set up our 501(c)(3). As I grew accustomed to walking the walk, I began to feel more empowered. No matter how many people stared or gawked, I felt like a warrior. I now had a purpose that was much greater than myself. My long years of suffering had perfectly prepared me for this new mission in life.

At parties, when someone turned to me and asked, "What are you up to these days, Celia?" I was proud to explain about my volunteer work on the burn unit and the mission of the newly formed Moonlight Fund. It turned out that the topic was a complete conversation stopper. People would break eye contact and abruptly change the subject. Some were so unnerved that they simply walked away. Again and again, I saw the degree to which people were uncomfortable with even the mention of burns.

For the first time in my life, I was building something outside myself for the benefit of others, not just being the fierce mama bear caring for myself or my own children. I had been so consumed with ensuring that my children had all the things I never did, I hadn't focused on what I could do for people outside my family. It was scary, it was overwhelming at times, it was a leap of faith—but the deeper I went, the more I realized how intensely rewarding it was to make a difference. Whether my contributions were small or large, it was and still is incredibly rewarding to help those whose lives are affected by burns.

As I continued to volunteer on the burn unit and work my way into the hearts of the medical and psych staff, I was allowed to accompany patients to the debriding showers. There I worked side by side with them as the medical staff undertook the grueling physical process of literally scrubbing skin off their patients. As the nurses performed their duties, I focused on the patients' eyes. I'd talk them through the punishing procedure by mentally helping them escape to a more peaceful place, if only in their minds. But as I walked with patients farther and farther along the recovery journey, I became increasingly—and uncomfortably— aware of how very few social services supported them when they needed them most. These were brave-hearted, hard-fighting survivors. Their needs were clear, but there were no resources to meet those needs.

I accompanied patients through each new challenging step, and fought side-by-side to get them what they needed. One of the patients was

Henry Coffeen III, a great big character with a great big heart. He was burned when his aerobatic plane caught fire and he was forced to eject. I spent a considerable amount of time with him, his wife Emily, and their family. We remained in touch after he left the hospital and during one conversation, I shared my frustration with the appalling lack of resources available for burn survivors. As much as I tried to solve problems, offer support, and address needs, I was continually faced by a lack of resources, funds, and very little help. Henry and I began to discuss how a nonprofit could be a more effective way to rally these desperately needed resources.

Once we had the idea and Dick helped us get going, there was no holding back. Henry, an avid pilot, said, "Let's host an airshow to raise money!" In a few short years, that airshow grew to host nearly twenty thousand people and was considered to be the airshow with the best talent in the U.S.

Ever since I was a little girl, I've never been afraid to dream big. But back then, I couldn't imagine that someday we'd help more than ten thousand people in the first twenty years of our foundation's work. This is thanks to our dedicated staff, volunteers, and our amazing partners and supporters who've donated money and/or services. Today Moonlight Fund is the largest nonprofit that provides direct financial support to burn survivors and their families, and we've received amazing recognition at all levels for the work we do.

And yet there was a price to pay. This particular passion and charitable cause did not sit well with Dick's socialite friends. My other interests—horses and golf—made for pleasant enough chitchat at parties and at the country club. And, of course, supporting charities—if only in the form of writing checks—was regarded as perfectly fitting and proper. But not this. Not hands-on work among the sights, smells, and sounds of the burn unit that were as foreign to these beautifully dressed people as the moon.

It grew harder and harder for me to answer the casual query, "What have you been up to lately, Celia?" My passion and my heart screamed to speak about what was most important to me, about the real reason I found direction and meaning. But invariably when I mentioned my work with burn survivors, the topic was quickly changed, an awkward silence arose, or the inquirer found an excuse to physically escape.

Just as I had been ostracized as a kid for my burns, now I was ostracized as an adult for assisting burn survivors. Although Dick supported me in my work, I think even he was a bit puzzled by the reaction of our friends. And in the social circles we moved in, there was only complete confusion, if not downright disdain and rejection. In all my conversations where the topic came up, not once did someone say, "That's really great that you are doing that work," or "Thanks for your commitment."

Burns are a taboo subject to just about anyone who hasn't been directly touched by them, but I think for this crowd it was something even more striking, really a demographic issue. Workplace hazards, home living conditions, abuse and neglect all play a part in burn injuries. It almost seemed that in this carefully curated environment, where everything was devoted to beauty and good taste, there was a sense of "Burns don't affect our sort of people, the pretty and affluent people. Only 'they' get burned." And, statistically, that is a fact.

Today, in the aftermath of two very long and very dreadful wars, I think attitudes have evolved somewhat, and there is a slow but growing acceptance of burn survivors, many of whom are warriors in both the military and as survivors. But during my time among that elite social set, the subject was very much taboo. My work led to social casualty and eventually my marriage became a casualty too.

I had thrown myself headlong into supporting and promoting Moonlight Fund and our mission. I was so very grateful to Dick for his support and for giving me the means to start the Fund, but in the end, I was so consumed by my work that I neglected our marriage. Each time I meant to reach out to Dick, to carve out time for him, something would interrupt—a phone call from the unit, another night spent at a patient's bedside, another call or visit to a potential donor. My obsession with assisting others cost us dearly, and it finally tore us apart. I simply did not have enough love or sympathy for anything outside my obsession. I did, however, carve out time for my children. I didn't miss a football game, dance recital, a corps event or a teacher meeting. I was determined to be "super mom."

There came a day when I asked Dick if I might enjoy a sabbatical. He agreed and set about finding some lush spas within hours of San Antonio. I wanted something different. I wanted to get away, in the middle of nowhere, just me and my dog, far from people, noise and the confusion of life. I remembered that a client of his had purchased a stunning, out-of-the-way place in west Texas. I had a chance to enjoy learning more about Cibolo Creek Ranch when it was featured in Architectural Digest and found its combination of rugged and remote grounds with luxury digs quite appealing. During a chat with Henry, my Moonlight Fund co-founder, who had recently visited the ranch, I knew I was destined for this remote location. A nine-hour drive of endless highways, far from home, with very few people, was just the type of adventure I was searching for. I fell in love with the landscape, the staff, the wildlife and the stars. While there I met several other guests, including Steven and his fiancé, Heather. Steven, a screenwriter, had chosen this peaceful, out-of-the-way spot to work on one of his screenplays. We fell into an easy friendship and enjoyed the days by the pool and nights filled with adventure, including viewing the Marfa lights. A few days into my stay, it was just the three of us and we awoke to something that can never be forgotten. The manager ran into the breakfast area stating that a plane had just flown into one of the twin towers. There was only one television on site and that was located in the owner's suite, which thankfully, I had access to. Shortly after turning it on I saw the second plane fly into the tower. The ranch manager was doing his best to persuade us all to stay. I had a different plan. I ran to my room, threw open the back of the Range Rover and began throwing my luggage and clothing in, I was going home, to be with my family and no one was going to stop me. I knew there would be no way for Steven and Heather to return to L.A. They would need to be someplace safe where Steven could communicate with his daughter back in L.A. So, I invited them to my home and off we went, on an eerie and long journey.

Once home, I was relieved to be with Dick, Hillary and the boys. Steven and Heather spent eleven days with us and just like the rest of the nation, we were glued to the television and took note of the skies void of any commercial air traffic. We did our best, dining out each night, sharing life stories and enjoying our fair share of wine, yet the mood was somber and overwhelming; 9/11 changed the world and would ultimately change the course of my life. As the war ensued, I found myself caring for hundreds upon hundreds of burned military members, many of whom did not survive. The Moonlight Fund was no longer a "hobby" or a "good deed"; it was now a vital part of caring for our nations heroes.

I began working more hours and obsessed over just how to raise the funds needed to care for so many people. Although the military provided many benefits, there were still needs for both the burn survivors and their family members. The combination of my work and my selfish, self-centered ways were taking me down a path to destruction and both my children and I would soon be paying a high price.

Dick and I agreed to divorce, and I wanted very little in regard to support or possessions. The one thing I did request was that he continue to cover the tuition costs at the high-end prep schools the children were attending. Dick had grown close to my children and assured me he would remain a part of their lives. Had I gotten greedy, I would have jeopardized those relationships and that was something I was unwilling to do, not for any amount of money. I left my big life, my big home, and moved to a home in the country. Dick remained in the children's lives for some time. By this time Hillary had begun calling him "daddy" and it warmed my heart to see her joy when Dick would roll up the drive to collect her for the weekend or dinner out.

But as he rejoined the dating scene, the children of an ex simply didn't fit. I know that he loved them, but the pressure placed on him by the women he dated became too much for him and he began to slowly exit their lives. He was the only father Hillary had ever known. Regardless, I found myself lying to her when asked why she hadn't seen daddy in so long. I'd explain away his absence with excuses of his work taking him away on travel or stating, "You know how busy he is." I lied and lied, and my heart broke more than I can describe.

But then, one day, little Hillary looked up at me with the understanding eyes of an old soul. She knew he was not coming to see her, take her for the weekend, spend a holiday, or enjoy a nice dinner. He was gone from her life. I could feel her heart breaking. As time progressed, Dick sought me out for the occasional date and things were very up and down. He spoke of getting back together, yet he'd fall in and out of my life. The pain I saw my children suffer, feeling rejected and forgotten, affected me, and I knew I could never have a future with Dick. I never felt any anger towards him, as these were natural changes. Yet my children's pain became my own, and I will never forget the last time he rang me on my cell phone. I was in my arena riding one of my horses alongside a student. He asked me out for dinner and when I responded, "Just as friends," and he said, "No it's a date." And with that, it all ended.

Hillary and me, Christmas, Wisconsin, 1994

*My assistant Cindy and me,
working a VanHolten's trade show*

Dick and me, ready for a night out

Having a bit of fun

Haydn and me at the cathedral of
St. John the Divine on our wedding day

It truly touched my heart that Dick
took up skiing for me

Attending TMI's
Military Ball with
Justin and Jarred

Me and Dick

Carrying on my mother's traditions. Christmas was always special and full of joy and surprises.

Marrying Dick, with Justin and Jarred looking on

TMI football days with Justin (left)

My mother and my sons during a trip to Hilton Head Island

Taking Christmas to an entirely new level

Justin, friend Tony Lupo, and Jarred. Looking awesome for another TMI event

Dick, the children, and me in our backyard

Dick and me with Heather and Steven

Chapter Six
Inspired

What a privilege, what a day

I was at my best, I was dancing with my worst, I was six feet from falling

I loved what I was doing, I have forgotten that day and lost my way

Here, I remember, I am allowed the gentle information that will help make me whole

Thanks to my guides, light and peers, I begin to understand my tragedy and be at one with myself.

I summon the universe, the stars and the moon, my guides and my light

Ben—Early Inspiration for Moonlight Fund

In the heat of July, a new patient arrived. Ben was one of the young ones. In his case, his burns were the result of a freak car accident. He had burns over thirty-four percent of his body and every reason to survive—or so we all believed. I spent day after day with his family as unspeakable heartbreak hit us. The bad developments came in waves. Skin grafts were rejected and infection set in.

On the burn unit, so often it's not the burns that will kill you, it's the infections—they are the kiss of death. Once a patient's infection sets in, it can kill like a tidal wave, roaring through room after room, patient after patient, spreading like a wildfire that has made a vicious deal with the devil. I held Ben's mother in my arms as we heard the awful news, and I could physically feel the absolute tearing apart of her heart. It tore through her, and then through me. All too soon, it was over.

But this family had stuck with me and with Ben through it all. I took all that courage and inspiration and funneled it into my desire to help others through the Moonlight Fund. To this day, Ben's family is a big part of all I do and I make sure Ben's legacy lives on. I made a promise then that every check made out to a burn survivor would have Ben's initials discreetly added. Twenty years, several million dollars and thousands of checks later, I still honor his memory each time Moonlight Fund assists one of our fighting survivors.

Crossing the Threshold

Years before meeting Ben and his family on the unit, I had my very first conversation with the director of the burn unit, Colonel Libby Bryant and I remember it being less than promising. I had come into the Brooke Army Medical Center to make an impassioned plea to volunteer on the burn unit. Having recently given up my career, I had some extra time on my hands. The life of a country club wife has its perks, yet, I found myself with a void. I needed to do something of purpose and I thought volunteering on the burn unit would keep me busy and perhaps provide a good service to others. She listened intently, yet her response was firm and immediate. "We do not allow volunteers on that unit."

Her reasons were crisp and direct; risks of infection were high enough with only medical professionals and families in residence, and Infection Control would never permit the presence of more outsiders. The psychological toll would be more than a volunteer, however well-meaning, could bear. The medical staff had their hands more than full attending to the needs of the patients and their families and couldn't take on the added burden of making sure volunteers were doing good and not causing harm.

But my vision of what I might do to make a difference in these lives and their families was very strong, and we continued to talk. She must have started to form her own vision of how I could help because she said, "I'd like you to meet a couple of our burn survivors, they're Vietnam War veterans." And that was how I met Chuck and David, the co-founders of Texas Burn Survivors.

They were very tough on me in those interviews, which turned out to be just the first of many equally tough conversations over the course of several months. We burn survivors are fiercely protective of our people, because we know just how much fear, suspicion, and misunderstanding they will face among the uninitiated. I was also asked to meet with several members of the burn unit team, and they were tough as well. Yet, I had set a course and was determined not to be persuaded to give up or give in. There was something calling my name and I was hell bent on finding my purpose.

But in the course of those conversations with Chuck, David, and the burn unit medical staff, I must have said something right. Not long after, Colonel Bryant arranged for me to meet with senior military members tasked with overseeing the burn unit. Once again, I think the power and clarity of my vision saved the day. Finally, the day came and Colonel Bryant gave me a chance, taking me to meet the lead nurse on the step-down unit, along with some of her staff.

A full range of emotions played across the lead nurse's face and I could see her turning over urgent questions in her mind. Who was this young thing, and what business did Celia have here? Why on earth would the colonel bring her here? Was Celia sent as a mole to keep an eye on things for Colonel Bryant? I set my jaw and looked her straight in the eye, not in a challenging way but to convey my determination.

She gave a slight smile and led me down the hall to meet my first patient. This poor soul had tried to commit suicide by setting herself on fire. She had such severe damage to her arms and legs that all four limbs had been amputated. What remained of her was gruesome, even to someone with absolute nerves of steel. I committed to coming in three days a week from that day forward, and I kept my word.

My credibility with the staff and my passion to serve became clear over time. The staff confided that they had assigned me their most heartbreaking cases. Initially, they thought I'd turn out to be a well-meaning but lightweight amateur, and they'd never see me again. My tenaciousness and fierce commitment finally won their trust, a sacred gift I cherish to this day. I stayed with this patient, my first case and a truly tough one. I even followed her to rehab and continued my visits with her there. Her life, painful enough before her suicide attempt, was even more so now, and six years later she made another suicide attempt. This time she succeeded.

In addition to my thrice-weekly commitment, I also spent many holidays on the unit because I know just how hard those times are on patients and their families. The unit became my second home, a place where I could have an impact—sometimes small, sometimes large. My passion matured from a vague insistent spark to a steady, focused guiding light, and I became part of the team. In a flattering vote of confidence, Colonel Bryant invited me to attend a week-long training session they required of all incoming burn unit medical staff, and I accepted with pride. It was incredibly helpful and inspiring, and I learned so much that made me a more effective volunteer, as well as a more valued member of the team.

Two of the first patients I worked with were badly burned when their plane lost power and crashed, hitting the tanks at a gas station. The plane exploded on impact and although the pilot, his female passenger, and the pilot's son managed to exit the aircraft, the pilot and passenger were both badly burned, in excess of seventy percent of their bodies. One survivor, Cassandra, was special—a devoted single parent with a thriving career.

Although now her life lay in the balance. I convinced the staff to allow her a visit with her children, which at the time was prohibited. I was on the unit when her two sons and daughter saw their mother for the first time. I vividly recall the shock and pain on their young faces.

So moved by Cassandra's plight, I increased my hours on the unit to spend more time with her and I made sure that I was present to be with her on surgery days. After the procedures, back in her room, I remember looking down at her after one skin graft in particular. Her chest bore the scars of newly harvested tissue. I also recall another visit we spent together with her physical therapist, Stuart Campbell. As he guided her down a quiet hall, taking her fist steps in months, the pain on Cassandra's face was clear. It was tough to see such a strong woman barely able to move and with tears in her eyes. That first step, for all patients, was always a painful path to progress.

The day finally arrived for Cassandra to leave and enter rehab, and as things so often do on the unit, the decision was made quickly. I had just enough time to race up to the unit for a hug and a goodbye. Before she left for the rehab facility, I contacted a friend who owned a high-end shop and asked if he had a lovely hand mirror in stock. Could he possibly get a courier to bring it to me on the unit? He did just that. After I helped Cassandra unwrap the mirror, I held it up for her and said, "This mirror will always remind you of just how beautiful you are."

Inspiration and Despair

The more I got to know the many men, women, and children in the burn unit, the more I came to admire their tenacity and courage in the face of terrible loss and unthinkable obstacles. One of my early patients, Joe, was from the Rio Grande Valley in South Texas. I was with him as he progressed through his physical therapy and when he was preparing for discharge to return home. I worked closely with his caseworker. I offered to help organize not only his transportation home, but also, his ongoing medical care.

Just days before Joe was scheduled to be discharged, I was spoke with him about going back to his city. I asked if he was set up to continue his physical therapy and to further his recovery with occupational therapy. He had only begun the process of healing and ongoing treatment was paramount to his realizing the best possible recovery.

His response was brief. "I don't have insurance and we can't find a facility to take me. I won't be getting PT or OT."

The implications sank in and my heart was in my throat. Without the right rehabilitative care, his future was grim. He'd invariably be back for more painful surgeries that would only extend his long and arduous recovery. How could there be nothing in place to ensure he got the care he needed? Nothing to give him a chance to return to some semblance of his life before?

As I had done so many times before, I was determined not to let an obstacle derail me from my mission—in this case to help a patient to whom I was very committed. I was determined to help Joe achieve his full potential in recovery.

I went straight to our lead caseworker, Katie Tyrell, to ask what nonprofits or assistance groups we could tap into. Her response was another unwelcome jolt: There weren't many. One small group offered a bit of assistance for patients in need, but they provided $200 per patient at the most, and then only to a select few patients because their resources were limited. Needless to say, $200 won't get you in the door to a good rehab center, much less provide the sustained services any patient would need.

I asked Katie if I could try to get Joe some additional help, and she was more than willing to have me roll up my sleeves and dive in. I began researching online, and then picked up the phone and made calls to any organization anywhere that might offer help. Each conversation was more discouraging than the one before. Either the help they offered was so small that it was essentially useless, or they had specific constraints—geographic location, need, age, etc.—that made Joe ineligible.

I was profoundly shaken. How could there be absolutely no resources to address a need that was clearly significant? In this generous-hearted country, there seem to be nonprofits focused on just about every condition under the sun, and yet there was nothing for Joe. I was desperate to help him and damned determined.

All I could do for Joe was to hang tough with him and his family, and as I feared, things did not go well for him. I felt heartsick and frustrated. That was my frame of mind when I fell into a conversation with another one of my patients, Henry Coffeen III. He was recovering from burns to over thirty percent of his body. Henry had been rehearsing for an aerobatic airshow when his plane caught on fire and he was forced to eject. It was this event that changed our lives forever. It was during this visit with Henry when the first conversation of many laid the foundation for what was to become my life's passion.

A Glimmer of Moonlight

By heartbreaking coincidence, not long before Henry crashed his plane, his home was horribly damaged in one of Central Texas's feared flash floods. But Henry was a bigger-than-life man with boundless energy, who had channeled his creative passions into building successful businesses and into one of the most active lifestyles I've ever known. At the time of his discharge, his doctors advised him that he would need follow-up surgeries on his hands for releases of the scar tissue. True to form, Henry went home and spent the summer water-skiing at his river house. This activity not only relaxed and energized him but it had the added benefit of releasing the scar tissue that had tightened on his hands.

Henry's tenacious spirit won out and he never needed additional surgery on his hands.

I always like to say that Henry is bigger-than-life, and this period of his life was no exception. In true Texas fashion, he proved himself to be one of the boldest, funniest, smartest, and most willing-to-take-a-risk men I have ever known. In business, he has a true Midas touch. And he's married to a striking beauty who's as smart and talented as she is lovely.

As I confided in Henry about my frustrations and dead ends regarding funding for the further treatment of burn survivors, his response was characteristically bold and big: "Let's do an airshow and start a nonprofit!" At the time, he owned a small airport in nearby Seguin, Texas; so we did just that. As I look back on our humble efforts, I realize that at the time I had not a clue that this would become my life's mission. I wish that at that time I had realized the ride I was in for. I would have certainly fastened my seat belt.

As I've said, my husband Dick used his position as a senior partner at Ernst & Young to get the time and expertise donated to set up the nonprofit entity. And, of course, he also generously provided the seed money. I am grateful to this day for the support and understanding Dick showed me and his part in founding an incredible nonprofit. It was a true leap of faith, to cofound a nonprofit. I had no experience, just my gut instinct and his unfailing support.

I also tapped into the expertise of the burn unit staff to help develop our mission and founding principles. I wanted their help in defining what specific needs we would address. Ben's family, with whom I still stayed in close touch, helped us create a website and supported us in every other way they could. It was exhilarating and inspiring to see how quickly and effectively this powerful set of stakeholders converged to support Henry's and my vision of Moonlight Fund: legal and accounting executives, burn survivors, medical professionals, and Ben's family, people who knew the pain that a burn injury can render on the burn victim's loved ones. We had a winning team and these founding efforts would impact the lives of 10,000 burn survivors in its first twenty years.

From Vision to Reality

We hosted our very first fundraiser at Henry's Seguin airport. More than three-hundred family and friends attended, and it was the first thrilling chapter in what became an annual tradition. By the sixth year, we'd outgrown the Seguin facility and moved to the larger New Braunfels airport, where they even extended the runway to accommodate our planes and built an air control tower. Attendance over the next three years grew to almost twenty thousand people. Our event was widely considered to have the best aerobatic airshow talent in the U.S. and through our connection with a Texas congressman, we were also bringing in the military's top pilots and planes. Not only did the airshows raise thousands of dollars, they were an incredible venue, allowing us to raise public awareness about the needs of burn survivors.

As time passed, that particular fundraiser format no longer made sense for us. Henry relocated to Fort Worth, a couple of hundred miles to the north. This was too far away to effectively coordinate the event.

As the U.S. military engagement in Iraq and Afghanistan deepened, the number of people filling up our burn unit rapidly increased, many of them with devastating injuries. More and more of my time was spent on the unit. Three days a week were not enough. I was faced with a huge decision. I only had so much energy, and the strain of a large fundraiser coupled with the increased needs on the burn unit were becoming incredibly difficult to balance. In the end, I chose to be bedside with our patients and in the waiting rooms with their families. I did not have the time, energy or heart to care for them and also host such a large fundraiser.

Having moved past the airshow as our signature funding source, I began to apply for grants. At the time, I had no experience in that area. I soon discovered that grant writing is a unique discipline that requires specialized expertise and a broad range of skills. But my way is to jump in fearlessly, learn fast, and get better quickly. I followed through with this mindset, knowing how badly we needed resources to execute our mission and tackled the process head-on.

I hired a grant writer on contract and worked with her to develop three different grant applications. Not a single one came through for us, I'm sorry to say. I was heartbroken and desperate to find a way to sustain funding. Having worked with the grant writer side-by-side—plus having done my own research on the art and science of grant writing—I decided to save any future expense and write the next grant application myself. I sought $98,000 from the San Antonio Area Foundation, to fund support and recovery retreats for our patients and their families. It was well above the amount we'd asked for in the first three applications, but my rationale was that if I wanted to think big about our retreat program, I'd better *ask* big. I could not have completed this task without the help of Sandie Paloma-Gonzalez. She worked for the San Antonio Area Foundation and was in charge of the grant applications at that time. She took me under her wing and walked me through the process. I remain forever grateful to Sandie, for had she not offered me such kind and generous support, I doubt I'd ever have written another grant. Today, I write an average of thirty grants a year. It's tough work, long hours, zero pay and the most rewarding job I've ever had.

It was an unbelievable thrill when the grant came through—the entire $98,000 I'd requested. These funds allowed us to introduce our award-winning retreat program. I am still writing grants, though thankfully I've had support in recent years from my daughter, Hillary. Our success rate is quite good. But then again, I think we fulfill such a special and important mission that we rightfully stand out among all the applicants. Of course, the need never stops, and most of the grants are relatively small, so it's a never-ending process. Needless to say, grant writing is a necessity related to my "real" job, which is to provide support to our patients, as well as supporting families in the burn unit and beyond.

A Labor of Love

So much of what I do isn't pleasant. I get down close to our patient' faces and talk them through things they physically cannot do. I spend time with them during their debridement and physical therapy, and we chat about a pretty place in their mind. I recall this place for them, getting so close to their face that I can taste their tears. I can still hear their screams and can still smell the scent of absent or decaying flesh.

At first I would go home, pour a glass of wine, and wander out to sit by the pool, staring into the distance, just trying to process everything that had happened during the day. Sometimes I'd be there for hours, too numbed to even think of doing anything else. But from the beginning, this whole aspect of my life has felt like part of a bigger plan. I play my part, I move forward, I pour my passion into my patients' suffering and rehabilitation day after day. It's more rewarding than anything I ever imagined or experienced. I knew that this part of my life was growing and overshadowing everything else: my experience as a proud partner of Dick who was by his side at social events; my relationships within and outside my family; my other hobbies and interests. Yet there was something so compelling about this work that I threw myself in headlong and have never looked back.

I believe that this is my destiny. There have been many, many occasions when I felt I just could not go on. I was exhausted—physically, financially, emotionally—and tried very hard to step away. Henry moved on with his busy life and although he remained supportive of our efforts, he simply does not have the time to be involved. I was on my own for many years of this endeavor, and there have been many days when it nearly killed me. I have come to see that, ultimately, I did not have a choice. This is who I am and Moonlight Fund is what I'm meant to bring to the world. And for all the hard work, the exhaustion, and the frustration, I love, love, love my patients and their families. In return, they give me far more than I can ever give them. They inspire me with their fighting spirit, their grace, and their generosity. They give me a reason to get out of bed, a reason to carry on when I think I have no reserves and no more resources. They give hope and meaning to each other, to me, and to those around them. They are the reason for every decision and choice that I make. They are the true heroes and true warriors.

The Face of Moonlight Fund

My experience with Moonlight Fund has convinced me that we have to put a "new face" on the abstract and sometimes negative idea of burn survivors. Well, my face is the only one I've got, so that is what I've used. I went to meeting after meeting, and event after event to promote our mission and raise awareness of our patients and the work we do with and for them. I was willing to use every connection I had—and my connections' connections—to get a foot in the door. I had to be the voice and the face for all those who are unable to share their own and I prayed endlessly that God would give me the strength to carry this mighty task.

My message is urgent: We must all retrain our hearts and our eyes to see not just the struggle and pain of those who have endured so much, but also to see their beauty and their mighty, mighty hearts. I know it is not an easy message. It's also not one that people digest readily, flipping their behaviors for the asking. So, I keep going and going.

In keeping with our mission-focused philosophy, our overhead remains purposely low, and we pour every dollar possible into serving our patients and their families. I work pro bono in an office located in my home. Our programs are crafted around patients' specific needs, which vary widely. And our reputation is, I am proud to say, absolutely stellar. Our patients and their families will tell you of the profound impact we have on their lives and those of their families. By 2012, we were recognized with the Fisher House/ Newman's Own Foundation Award for excellence, naming Moonlight Fund the top nonprofit in the nation for our healing retreat program.

This award was presented to me at the Pentagon by General Martin E. Dempsey, chairman of the Joint Chiefs of Staff, in a ceremony that was incredibly moving and that I will remember for the rest of my life. When I was asked to speak at the Pentagon, I was so very honored to speak in a truly hallowed spot, the Hall of Heroes, on the building's awe-inspiring main concourse.

Through the years many awards would follow, some for Moonlight Fund and others for me, recognizing my personal efforts on behalf of burn survivors. In the summer of 2016, I received a call from Dottie Wainwright, a member of the Daughters of the American Revolution, (DAR). I'd known Dottie for quite some time and she asked if I wouldn't mind if she nominated me for a DAR award. I was so taken by surprise! I could not fathom how such a prestigious organization would want to give me an award and it warmed my heart to know that Dottie thought so much of my work. Dottie was and is a true patriot and worked selflessly to improve the lives of our wounded military members. Yet, here I was, one year later reading her email stating I had indeed, been selected to receive the DAR Distinguished Citizen Medal. She went on to say that this was to be unannounced until the night of the event set for March of 2018. I asked if I might share the news with Randy, since he would need to make plans to be home and I knew that, just like the award at the Pentagon, I wanted him by my side. Dottie agreed and asked that several of the wounded military members Moonlight Fund had assisted also attend. As

I shared the news with Randy I could feel his pride not only for the award, but also for the work we do.

While awards and recognition are nice, what brings me the most profound satisfaction is helping those less fortunate. As I work in my home office, surrounded by our many trophies, the photos of my children and patients and the stacks of work to do, I must pause, breathe in the last twenty years and pray I have more to give. I've made a lot of sacrifices over the years, including selling one of my beloved horses and emptying my personal bank accounts to keep us going in lean times. But my passion for our mission is never in question, and I'm strengthened in my resolve every single day by our amazing and beautiful burn survivors and their family members. I'm also very focused on structuring the organization to withstand the test of time. It cannot succeed long-term if it's "Celia's baby." So, in our governance, planning and development, I think ahead to the next generation of leadership and the one beyond that.

I include my children in many of our events, from emptying trash cans at the airshows to hauling boxes at our ladies day events; they were all expected to work and contribute their time. Yet, I am acutely aware that my children made their fare share of sacrifices for my "work," both financially and of my time. I found less and less time to be with them, so I slept less, reorganized my schedule, and reminded myself that Justin, Jarred and Hillary were the most important three beings in my life. I also wanted the opportunity to visit my sister, who remained so dear to me. I began to ask my board members and co-founders for more help, I sought out volunteers because I simply could not carry the load on my own shoulders any more. The needs are so great and far-reaching, yet the amount of assistance available to burn survivors is so little. I pray each day that change comes and that more help be made available here in the U.S. to burn survivors and their family members. I also pray that it does not take another war to open peoples' eyes and move their hearts.

My daughter, Hillary, preparing to go up in a Pitts at one of our airshows

My son, Justin, and me working a Moonlight Fund event

Humble beginnings: My co-founder, Henry Coffeen III, announcing at our 1st airshow as I watch

Justin, Hillary, Jarred, and me

Justin, Hillary, and me in Santa Fe

Hillary and me in Belize

My son, Jarred, in his TMI Corps of cadets
uniform — I was so proud of him

Precious visit with my sister, Audra

Hillary and me at the beach

Chapter Seven

Safety in the Moonlight

How often does the moon glow full

Yet, you noticed her only once

She was there for you, each month

As a reminder of the warm arms that hold you from above

And keep you safe from the harm below

You barely noticed your illuminated footsteps that night or the way the leaves on the trees seemed to shine

When she hung crescent with the star, did you take in her beauty, as if admiring a piece of art?

The moon, she is omnipresent, the one thing you can count on each day to shepherd you down this path of life. Consider her your creature, for she watches over you daily

People often ask why we chose the name Moonlight Fund and how it came to be. At the time we were founding the organization, I owned a horse named Northern Moonlight. One day, while I was driving, I thought of him briefly and the name clicked—just the right insight and foreshadowing. I thought about how we, as burn survivors, feel safest in the moonlight, and I rolled the thought over in my mind that a nonprofit for burn survivors should be "safe" and protective. You may never see a burn survivor, although there are thousands living among you. That is because we isolate. Part of that isolation is shopping at 24-hour Walmarts, where we are safe from the harmful rays of the sun and the prying eyes of others. In the softer light, our scars are less jarring, less likely to provoke stares and startled reactions from those around us. In the moonlight, we're most comfortable leaving the quiet and safety of our homes to go out and transact our business and get on with the demands of daily life, post-trauma. Simply put, we find *safety* in the moonlight.

Burns are so terrifying to others that people recoil and reject, even if that's not their initial intention. Burn survivors often move invisibly past us, shopping or running errands only at night, hiding from gaping stares or averted glances. In those late hours, accompanied by only a handful of those they love and trust, burn survivors find security and acceptance. Only in the moonlight do they find safety. And Moonlight Fund exists to give them that love, trust, safety, and acceptance in every aspect of their lives and to the fullest possible extent.

Our award-winning retreats offer such peace and solitude, not only for the burn survivor, but also the family members. Hosted at the Silver Spur Ranch in Bandera, Texas, or far-away locations such as our caregivers retreat in Puerto Rico. Far from the outside world, we are free to be ourselves. Old friendships are reunited, and new ones come to life. The children and spouses of burn survivors find a common bond and we become family, in a way that is tough to describe yet easy to embrace. There's no need to cover up scars, fabricate a story or explain away the accident. Days spent on horseback and long evenings over a game of cards provide the perfect backdrop for recovery and fun. Staff at Silver Spur Ranch have become a part of our extended family, not only remembering names, but also, who likes grilled cheese at midnight, our favorite horses and how we like our steaks cooked. It's more like one big family reunion than a retreat. As new attendees enter the fold, it's touching to see our established Moonlight Fund family take them in, gently introducing them to fellow attendees and activities. It doesn't take long for them to relax and warm up to the hospitality and love that envelopes them at these amazing events.

The results of being a burn survivor are wide-ranging and completely upends a person's life and the lives of those who love them. Each individual's experience is unique, of course, but for many of our patients the impact is profound and heartbreaking. Because of the very visible reminders, a burn survivor can never compartmentalize. The burns are there every day, and in everything they do. Burns are forever injuries to both the mind and the body.

Of course, the nature of our work means that we develop a very close personal bond with those we serve. At the same time, we have to preserve enough emotional distance to keep ourselves strong at the core for the next person and the one after that. It's a delicate balance, to care for someone and take them into your heart, while protecting your own heart and mind at the same time.

Our mission is to provide emotional, financial, and in-kind support, but the emotional support always comes first. We think beyond the immediate patient, to their families. I still stay in close touch with Jeanie, whose daughter, Amanda, a wing walker, suffered burns five years ago while performing in an airshow. I had promised Amanda I would look after her mother. Jeanie had already gone through enormous pain when she lost her husband just two years earlier, also in an aerobatic accident. And though her daughter was in a medically induced coma when I spoke to her, I know from extensive experience how much people hear and understand when they are in that state. I told her that I would be there for her mother. She left this world not long afterward, and I believe she left with peace of mind knowing that someone would be there for her mother through the long dark days to come.

That's just one example. I have so many people with whom I've stayed connected—bound as soulmates—after I've taken that very intimate journey with them on the hard path to recovery. It's a privilege to walk that path with them, and it's a journey that involves absolute trust and full commitment on both sides. The resulting relationship is so profound that nothing else in my life truly matches it. I carry the joy, the pain, the pride, and the power of the most remarkable people imaginable, and I am so much richer for it.

Along this journey I have often shared these experiences with my father. It may seem strange to some that I even speak to him, yet he is my father and I do love him. I am grateful for my burns, for without them I would not be on this mission of mine. I hold the strong belief that much of our life is pre-ordained and if that is a fact we are wise to make the best of our situation. With that said, my father's abusive ways carved a path to help thousands of people and that, in my eyes, is a beautiful thing.

Advocate for Thriving

Moonlight Fund has reached far beyond the individual journeys of burn survivors and their family members. Some of the work we do takes on systemic issues. For example, we have lobbied state and federal lawmakers to increase benefits for burn survivors, especially as the numbers continue to climb from our troops who face burn-inducing dangers in war-torn foreign countries. It's not unusual for someone suffering from a "big burn" to undergo thirty or more surgeries, and many times their insurance coverage is depleted. We've also gone head-to-head with veteran services and private insurance companies, demanding the highest level of benefits for our patients. Time and time again, I have stood against large entities, knowing that I am just Celia, yet I am mighty and powerful in my journey.

There is another systemic issue that is hard to talk about, but I want to address it. For many, many people, there is a gut-level physical revulsion to the scars that burn survivors carry. Because burns are so stigmatizing, people don't want to talk about it. In San Antonio, where there are many military burn survivors in recovery, there is more support and understanding than in other areas of the country. But when a burn survivor veteran goes back to his or her hometown, they are frequently shunned. That's why we want to move the needle on this issue—through awareness, support, and acceptance. We want to give every burn survivor the support and respect they deserve so they can recover and prosper wherever they are.

If we're going to succeed in our mission, we must put a new face on the world of burn survivors. At the same time, I recognize that we have to pull people in gently, at a pace they can accept. We must create an environment in which burns are looked at more kindly and with more understanding.

By the time I was four, my facial burn scars were no longer visible. However, my arm, chest, and buttocks still carry the story of my survival. I make it a point to no longer dress to try to cover them up. I've decided to live my life openly and honestly, which is so different from my childhood where I consciously and unconsciously disguised those scars. Yet, I will share that with each spring, when light clothing becomes the norm, I brace myself and find the strength to show who I am.

I'm not ashamed to use my face, my voice, or my story to open doors and get our message out into the larger world. I try to create a "soft" introduction to engage people and bring them into the world of burns, and gradually help them understand the need, look it straight in the eye, and find it in their hearts to assist us. I'm not ashamed to talk about the huge ropy scars across my buttocks where surgeons harvested donor skin to treat my burns and where my body reacted by developing hypertrophic scars.

Yet, I must confess that even after all these years, there is still a small part of me that feels the visible burn scars stigma. My own children grew up surrounded by burns. They attended summer camps where we hosted children on the journey to recovery, where our younger survivors could safely play and experience the normal activities and getaways of camp life without the gawking stares and intrusive questions. It's one of the great joys of my life that my two sons and my daughter truly do not see "a burn" or a "frightening" scar. They see the beauty of the person. They see an ordinary human being with all the strengths and flaws and hopes and fears that any person has—only with the heart to overcome challenges that most people, blessedly, will never have to face.

Moonlight Fund people are mighty and powerful. They are special. I believe that surviving burns and going through the rebuilding process all adds up to developing a purpose in your life in some way or another. Maybe you're a better parent. Maybe you're a more determined athlete. Maybe, like me, you've been led to a mission that you wouldn't have found otherwise, and you're blessed to wake up each morning knowing that you'll dedicate every resource you can muster to helping someone else. You will have an impact.

I try to help parents of burned children find an area in which the child is gifted or has a special interest. Then we focus on that area, not simply on the endless round of hospitalizations and painful procedures. Maybe the child will actually find more healing through piano lessons or baseball camp than through another agonizing surgery—a surgery that may not result in a significant quality of life change.

I often invite young burn survivors and the children of burn survivors to come visit my horses and Lilly the donkey at my ranch. We fall into easy discussions about the Friesian horse breed and Sicilian miniature donkeys. We let the children ride the animals and play in the arena. I've seen time and time again how these interactions brighten their eyes. Finally, they have something to engage their interest and humanity that doesn't involve medical procedures or therapy sessions!

It can be a balm for the family members as well. I suggested riding lessons for the daughter of a burn survivor. She'd initially felt overwhelmed and didn't see how she could cope when both her dad and dog were burned.

When their home had exploded, this girl, her brothers and mother had nothing. Clothing, toys and keepsakes were all gone and worse, their father was in critical condition on the burn unit. To this day, her riding lessons uplift and brighten her life. It also provides emotional relief to her mother, to see her daughter blossom in the horse arena.

The concept is very simple but powerful: Figure out what's right with the child, not just what's wrong.

On the Burn Unit: Becoming Part of the Family

Once I was accepted as part of the burn unit team, I found myself being pulled into caseworkers' offices and the nurses station, not only to discuss patients I might be able to help, but to be a safe and listening ear where they could vent. Even seasoned burn unit medical staff feel the stress of seeing so many people die, particularly during the first years of the wars in Afghanistan and Iraq. Back then, the unit was filled with seventeen- to twenty-three-year-olds. So many of them didn't make it. And of those who did, many were unrecognizable.

The caseworkers needed me to be there, as did the nurses, doctors and physician assistants. They all needed to talk. They trusted me. They described the horror and how it affected them. They shared how work had impacted their home life, and they shared the horrors of looking down at a human being that looked just like a fresh-skinned deer.

They worried because they needed to take antidepressants, yet they knew they couldn't perform their job without them.

"Every single one of us takes an antidepressant," a doctor once told me. And their faces told the stories of long hours, death, pain, and—oh— that smell.

Military nurses worried about losing rank if their commanding officer knew the toll this work took on them. So, they had no choice but to show up to work a job they didn't choose, and to spend whatever amount of time the military had allocated. I respect the commitment our military members make not only to this nation, but also to our wounded, many of whom have paid the ultimate price for our defense.

A Family Affair

About four years ago, my daughter, Hillary, who was then twenty-one, told me she wanted to dedicate herself to Moonlight Fund. I said, "No." I tried hard to dissuade her, to throw myself in the path and stop her from taking on the stress and the financial and emotional demands. I reminded her of the things our family has sacrificed for the fund: college educations for her and her brothers, the sale of my horses, marriages torn apart and near financial ruin were just a few of the things sacrificed for Moonlight Fund. But she was insistent, and I must say she inherited her mother's stubbornness and determination.

I threw her the most detailed grant application I could. It required very complex and extensive content and mind-numbing budget details. I was sure this would stop her folly. To my amazement, she turned the grant around in just a few days. She did an outstanding job.

Throughout her life, Hillary has proved to be an extremely gifted, intuitive and balanced young woman. She kept me going through all my struggles with self-medication, fear of commitment, and the deep-seated belief that I was unlovable. Together we explored arts, culture, travel—and love without limit.

Now we are a team professionally as well as personally. It's sometimes a challenge to work together, but it is ultimately rewarding. Today I appreciate how special it is to team up in this way. She's been exposed to so much and learned so much in her role as development director. She has co-written grants, developed complex fundraisers from the ground up, and accompanied me on travels near and far for public speaking engagements. She may not have a college degree, but she's gotten a wonderful education.

Hillary edits all our grant applications and works alongside me in the office with filing and record-keeping. I know it isn't fair, but I do expect more of her than I would of an ordinary employee. Hillary is a great editor and she has helped breathe fresh life (and an insistence on meticulous accuracy) into our grant writing. By nature, Hillary is a modest individual; her natural inclination is to be a behind-the-scenes person. But in her role as development director, she is propelled into a more interactive role and it's a delight to see her become more outgoing and publicly confident.

Perhaps the most rewarding part of Hillary becoming part of the Moonlight Fund family has been the strong ties she has made with many of our burn survivors and their family members. She is more like a sister to the wives and mother to many of the children. At retreats, it's Hillary who stays up till the wee hours of the morning and offers her ear and her heart to those who need to talk. She grew up in this world and she understands it like no other. She does not see scars. None of my children do and I'm grateful for that.

Speaking at the Amos House of Faith Fundraiser

Hillary working the booth at the American Burn Association Conference, 2016

Riding Northern Moonlight

Emotional reunion with Amanda's brother, pilot Matt Younkin

Late night card games are always popular at our retreats

Horses provide a large measure of therapy at Moonlight Fund retreats

Hillary with her brother, Jarred, at one of the galas she produced

My father continued flying well into his 70s — seen here with his Pitts

A visit with burn unit flight staff

Introducing Shilo Harris at our 20th Anniversary fundraiser, March 2018

Issac Gallegos, Hillary, me, and Shilo Harris

CHAPTER EIGHT

Libertad

The flames did not burn me

I was immune to the heat, only my heart skipped a long and languishing beat

I'm not lost, don't feel the pain

It is in this life that I will surely hope to gain

Love to others, pity to none

My heart I give to you all, my brothers, my world and my son

Spent this life living in shame

Thanks to the universe, for our spirits gain

Steady the light, I see it now.

To all those gone before me, I will bow

A Great Passion

Clearly, the last twenty years of my life have been intensely rewarding—and alternately frustrating, heartbreaking, and inspiring—through my work at Moonlight Fund with our amazing "family" of burn survivors. Long before the idea of Moonlight Fund began to take shape, I had a great passion. There was a love that carried me through, that one thing I would fight and die for without giving it a thought: horses.

When I was little, my mother had some truly stunning horses. Some of my earliest memories are of watching her, mesmerized, as she worked with these magnificent animals. There was one in particular that I vividly remember, a spectacular Morgan stallion named Stormy. I watched with fascination as my mother broke and trained this horse. To see the two creatures, human and horse, slowly build trust and connection across a deep divide, working together until they became one glorious, seamless unit of poetry in motion, touched me very deeply. As a small child, I felt lucky to get the occasional pony ride, but deep inside I wanted much more. I wanted to grow up and be just like my mother, a fearless master of magnificent equines.

After my father left, the luxury of maintaining horses quickly evaporated. But my longing to be around these creatures continued to gnaw at me. In an effort to be near them, I took a job one summer at a high-end horse farm. I mucked stalls, groomed horses, and watched longingly as, one by one, the little rich girls came out to ride and take lessons on these magnificent animals.

One day, one of these horses was restless and uncooperative. He was acting up, rearing and kicking out, frightening his young would-be rider as she readied for her jumping lesson. Her trainer kept insisting she mount the spirited fellow, but the girl's fear was palpable. She suddenly turned to me and said, "You warm him up."

I had not been on a horse in years, much less a highly trained, carefully bred hunter/jumper warmblood horse. I reached deep inside and plucked my "fearless badge" from the depths of my steely soul, and I took this wild man out into the arena. After watching riding/jumping lessons for months, I did the one thing I knew to do: Sit straight and lean towards the jumps.

This breathtaking horse must have sensed a kindred spirit in me because in just moments we were clearing jumps and somehow I stayed on, my heart leaping with each successive victory. Word about my prowess spread quickly at the stables and, from that point forward, I was the go-to person for warming up many of the horses. I saved up some of my precious dollars to buy a pair of rubber riding boots. The well-heeled girls who took lessons were quick to note that I did not have fine leather boots like their own, but to me it didn't matter. What mattered is that I never came off a horse, and I found the fear exhilarating.

Years later, I was still trying to fill empty spots in my soul. When I married Dick and, for the first time, had the means to indulge myself, he agreed to let me buy a horse. Dick was wealthy and he was generous, but because he knew very little about the horse world, he allotted me only $5,000. Anyone who's been in the world of horses knows that won't take you very far. I bought a thoroughbred off the track that fit within the budget. The horse, Northern Moonlight, only knew how to do two things, and they were to go fast and go left, making rides not only thrilling but also dangerous. I spent hours and hours with him and we learned a lot together. Over time a level of trust and understanding was established.

As I grew more involved with Moonlight Fund and with my horse, I felt my soul begin to heal. All those years of career success had brought a surface satisfaction to my life and my first taste of financial security since early childhood. But I still felt a restlessness and uncertainty that gnawed at me anytime I paused to catch my breath. As noted, my dedication to my burn survivors and their families cost me my marriage to Dick, but my life was finally beginning to find meaning and take shape at the most fundamental level.

My next marriage was to Jay Higuchi, a prominent pulmonary doctor in San Antonio. He knew about my passion for both Moonlight Fund and horses, and his generosity proved to be the mother lode of horse heaven for me. He allowed me to import two Friesians from the Netherlands to add to my existing mare, an Appendix American Quarter Horse. My mare, Lexell, was a very "hot" horse, meaning she was dangerous to ride or even to be around. But until that time, she was all that I could afford. Riding her was a thrill and I dearly loved her. Getting the Friesians was such a luxury because it meant I could ride on comparatively safe horses and focus on my love for riding, rather than trying to survive my mare's moods. My husband, Jay, had seen for himself how that mare got out of control, and it worried him.

Jay also indulged a long-held fantasy of mine and built me a full-blown arena and a show barn. I had carte blanche at the tack store to outfit my horses and myself with everything we desired. Word spread like wildfire in the close-knit horse community, and suddenly I was known for owning the "it" barn. Everyone with the means to do so wanted to either ride, board, or train there. It was a glorious period of my life, a dream come true for this hard-luck girl. I realize now I was only afforded this dream due to the love Jay bore me.

I regret that my self-absorption—in the horses and in Moonlight Fund— was in the end deeply unfair to my husband, and this marriage didn't survive. He was a kind and generous soul and certainly did not deserve the life I offered him. I was once again openly and completely committed to Moonlight Fund. As I've said, this calling has chosen me as much as I have chosen it, and there is no question where my true loyalty will forever lie.

On my own once again, piece by piece the castle in the sky fell away. First, I lost the barn and all its beautiful trappings. I made tough decisions in order to keep Moonlight Fund going during some lean years; I sold off my beloved horses. In addition, my doctors were pointing to my chronic, serious back issues and telling me that if I kept on riding I would permanently end up in a wheelchair, or even dead. Eventually the day came that I sold my last horse, Sansei—my baby and a valuable one at that. I donated the money to Moonlight Fund. My heart broke and remained broken for many years.

It was with as heavy a heart as I can remember that I finally gave away all my tack and riding clothes, the last vestiges of the horse-filled years of my life.

The One

After so many wrong turns with love, I finally found the right man. I first met Randy Belt in January of 2008 through a mutual friend, Pam Corbin. I was nonplussed upon meeting him, but Pam continued to ask if he had called. She was incredibly determined to find Randy the right woman. Eventually, Randy and I had our first date on February 12, 2008, our second on the fourteenth and our third, on my birthday the sixteenth. There was so much attraction, so much chemistry. For the first time in my life, I was willing to make adjustments to my own life for a man.

Randy's passion was hunting, so I knew I'd need to take up that hobby. I wanted to be a part of everything in his life. This delighted Randy; he'd been married numerous times and had never experienced the joy of a true soulmate, lover, and buddy. He and I were also very spiritually connected—he often commented that we must have been together in a previous life and would surely meet up again in the next. This was a once-in-a-lifetime love, and we simply could not function without one another. Hunting became one of our strongest bonds. We could be out in the wild for days, seeking the thrill of the hunt and never returning to civilization long enough to even shower.

Then, it all came crashing down. Randy left for a weekend rendezvous with one of his ex-wives. It was painful leaving him, but I did, I have more respect for myself than that. Until this, no man, husband or boyfriend had ever betrayed me in such a way and the experience left me shattered. The weeks dragged by, I busied myself with work yet I felt longing and hurt in my heart 24/7. Randy sent several short emails, "testing the waters," but I was resolute. I was not going back. I knew he had a hunting trip planned with his buddy Mike Corbin to Namibia and during that time, it was as if my body was transported to him. I felt close to him, almost with him. I could visually see the landscape of Africa and feel his breath on me. When he returned, I relented and we went out. Randy told me how he had felt in Africa, as if I was right there with him, just as I had felt. Once again, we were connected in a way that is tough to describe but easy to enjoy.

Until I'd met Randy, I'd had very little experience hunting and I am so grateful that he introduced me to the sport in a proper fashion. In short order, I felt every bit as passionate about hunting as I already did about riding. I lived and breathed it, and when I wasn't practicing at the range, I was glued to television shows on the sport, such as "Tracks Across Africa." Randy purchased a 308 Kimber for me with this incredible green Trijicon scope. I fell in love with that gun, its walnut stock, the way the weight felt against my shoulder, and the power at which it could kick me back.

As I generally do, I was focused on wanting to be the very best I could be. Randy's work kept him out of town, and on his monthly visits home we'd spend mornings at the range or hunt local Texas game to prepare for our own hunting trip to Africa. To be prepared for that trip with an expert marksman like Randy, I needed to be spot on. Randy's not only a gifted marksman, he's an ethical hunter, never wanting an animal to suffer. The accurate kill shot is very important.

He was tough on me, and when we had target practice, he was quick to call me out if I was performing to less than my capabilities. I can still see him walking towards the target and inspecting my shots, if they were not in a quarter group, he'd ask me, "What's wrong with you today?" That was fine with me because I respond well to tough love and I knew that if I were to hunt alongside an expert marksman such as Randy, I had better be at my best.

Accordingly, I excelled and became an extraordinary shot. Randy and I fished, hunted, worked the land, and drank together, often behaving more like two good old boys than husband and wife. Randy can make even the most wicked of swear words somehow sound sexy and we never tired of one another's company. I truly loved this man.

My reward for honing my sportsmanship and hunting skills was phenomenal indeed: Africa. Africa, each time that word rolls off my lips, I am transported back to that sacred land. When Randy told me that we were going there, I was equally excited and terrified as I prepared for the experience of a lifetime. Randy booked us the honeymoon cabana at Omatako, a hunting ranch in Namibia. He'd gone there the year before, hunting with his friends.

The location was beautiful and our cabana was remote, set far away from the rest of the compound. It was a thrill to walk out in the blackest night and have a herd of waterbuck staring right back at us. Equally thrilling was spending the afternoon between hunts watching a warthog and her young enjoying the water. One hundred fifty protected acres surrounded our place, making it possible to live among indigenous animals. The hunts were long and hard. We were up every day before sunrise, back in the afternoon for a break, and then back out at night. Randy and I hunted separately with our own PHs (professional hunters) for most of the trip, but, when we would hunt together, Randy's loving ways were ever evident as he allowed me shots on animals that would have typically been reserved for him. We also donated 4,000 pounds of meat to the local village; once again, Randy was thinking of others.

My doctor had warned me that the long flight might be quite painful due to my multiple back issues and prescribed a cocktail of pills to get me through. In preparation for just how tough it might be on me, we booked first class tickets with the hopes that the extra leg room and seating would spare me some pain; it didn't. I found myself on the floor, leaning over the seat, downing strong narcotics with a cocktail mixed in here and there. Nothing worked, but I made it and the rewards made the difficult trip worth it. Each day brought new record-breaking trophies, animals that are quite difficult to hunt in a dangerous land where the unexpected can show up at every turn. I reveled in the unimaginable excitement and I fell more deeply in love with Randy; we were truly soulmates.

The searing heat and sun are hard on burn survivors. While we were on the trip, I succumbed to the African weather, becoming quite ill from the heat. I stayed behind for two days to recuperate while the rest of the party proceeded with the hunt. On occasion, I'd venture out into the camp as the locals worked to iron my clothes, prepare meals, and care for their children. I was acutely aware that these proud people who once hunted the land and lovingly raised their children in age-old traditions had seen all of that taken from them over time. I thought about how the mighty dollar of the foreign hunters now ruled the land. These once independent people had become hired help. They worked in poor conditions at the whims of occupiers who visited, strutted around for a few days, and disappeared again, only to be replaced by the next group.

I also visited with the ranch owner, Elfie. Randy had hunted on her ranch the year before, and he told me about a pair of rescued cheetahs that Elfie cared for in a fifty-acre enclosure. One had been killed by a black mamba snake since Randy's last visit, so only one of these magnificent animals remained.

I asked Elfie if I might visit the cat and waited while she considered my request. After some thought, she agreed, but she laid down the ground rules. As I entered the enclosure, I saw nothing but acres of tall grass. I walked a few yards into the tall grass, stood very still, focused, and observed closely. Then I heard a sound—a low rumble like a deep cat purr, yet it was incredibly loud. I saw a steady ripple in the tall grasses that betrayed her path as she moved towards me. Suddenly like a mirage becoming real, she was in sight. I stood completely still, waiting for her to approach on her own terms in her own time.

I cannot adequately describe the feelings that rushed through me as I reached down and stroked that superb creature, a bewitching half-wild, half-affectionate work of incredible beauty. The thought that at any moment I could be her dinner made the entire experience even more thrilling.

Another deeply moving experience was our time among the giraffes. After a day of hunting, we came across a large herd of these hardy creatures, which we had no desire to shoot. I wanted to be with them, and I asked our PH to stop the truck. I stepped out slowly. These phenomenal animals average 2,800 pounds, and yet move with an agility and grace that seems impossible. As Randy and I approached, several of the youngsters acted like curious kids and moved quite near.

Suddenly, the bull giraffe appeared. While he was imposing, and left no doubt that he could more than assert his authority, he seemed to know that we were not a threat. We sat down and took in the incomparable African sunset, surrounded by these quiet, graceful, and utterly breathtaking creatures. I was with the man I loved and was certainly convinced that this was heaven. In that moment, I wanted to stay in that magical land and live among the indigenous animals and people. But in the end, I returned for the Moonlight Fund where I was needed by so many.

Unable to shake the spell of my time there, I wrote a piece on my trip, "Hunting Honeymoon," that was published by the Dallas Safari Club. The story and my record-breaking trophies ultimately caught the attention of Safari Club International, which reached out and asked if I would write a story for them to publish. Back in my familiar surroundings, I sat down to write the piece. As I did, I was flooded by the memories of my days with the people, the workers, the animals. I simply had to include what I observed—a people whose way of life has been stolen from them by the greed, appetites, and insatiable egos of hunters with money. I felt it was my duty to describe what I saw in full honesty and not to sugarcoat the reality. It did not surprise me that the story was never published.

Throughout the years of our marriage, Randy was unfailingly supportive of the Moonlight Fund and our mission. He was there for me and my patients at every turn, from loaning the fund money to get through tough spots, to helping with fundraisers. Many times he'd say goodbye to me, knowing I might not return for days when I'm needed in the burn unit. He took a personal interest in many of the survivors we help. Randy would take them hunting and fishing, or simply sit with them on the back deck and listen to all they needed to share.

I admit that I feared that he too would leave me—and who would blame him? Between my animals and my work at the fund, there was precious little left of me for others, including my own husband. We had come close to separating many times, but at the end of the day, our love for each other and our dedication to the work we do at Moonlight Fund carried us through. I hoped and prayed that we'd continue to be together in that spirit of love, strength, and commitment.

The fact that I do all my Moonlight Fund work pro bono is another complication that a lot of spouses might not have accepted. I was acutely aware of how I was part of a partnership, but I brought nothing to the table financially. It took a special partner to accept that the value of my work is measured by its impact on lives, not on mutual financial security. I continued to spend considerable time away from home, doing public speaking, to raise awareness of burn survivors, Moonlight Fund, abuse survivors, and our many worthy nonprofit sister agencies.

Randy never complained—he simply kept loving me like no else ever had—and I continued to spread my message. A message that goes out to all who may have things in their lives that hold them back or that may keep them from achieving their full potential, whether from a sense of fear or a lack of understanding. I urgently communicate that we each have the ability to rewrite the narrative of our tragedy, to pull strength from it and become better, more realized human beings.

For these and many other reasons, I continued to be grateful for Randy's understanding and support. To this day, whether day or night, the phone rings and I may be on calls for hours, or head out the door to care for a burned brother, not knowing when I will return. Randy's work took him around the world, which in some ways was a blessing because when he was gone I could spend countless hours working, riding my horses, or working the land.

One day, I was riding with a group of women, one of them asked, "How can you spend so much time away from your husband?" My response was swift and full of love. I said, "I'd spend a thousand days without him to have just one day with him."

My journey back to having horses in my life is one that continues to inspire gratitude from within me. After I sold my last horse, many years passed before I rode again. Over time, I was asked to work a few horses, and as destiny would have it, my husband saw this passion begin to burn again. He insisted that we build a barn. Today, I once again own my own horses. At first, I resisted the idea. After all, I was riding three horses for people who had hired me to work their animals. Because of this, I had horses in my life without the financial and emotional commitment of owning them myself. Randy knew, better than me that I needed some form of joy in my life, other than caring for burn survivors 24/7.

Deep down, the thought of having it all, and then facing the possibility of losing it again, was more than I could bear. But after six months of arguing Randy wore me down, and I agreed to design and build the barn. As it happened, the owner of one of the horses I'd been riding, a Friesian named Toranado, recognized the bond I'd built with him. She offered to sell him to me. I felt that bursting happiness in a place in my heart that had been empty for so long.

A few months later, my phone rang. I expected to hear about a new patient on the burn unit or an update on one of my Moonlight Fund patients. Instead it was Amie Paula, the woman I had sold my first imported Friesian to when I lost it all. This wonderful Friesian, Broer, had suffered an injury almost two years earlier. Together, Amie and Broer had ascended to some very high levels in the dressage ring, and Amie didn't have the heart to ask the horse for more after he'd undergone extensive surgery and months of rehab.

She had been offered a large sum for Broer. It was widely known that he could take anyone into a show ring and readily grab blue ribbons. But Amie loved him. After agonizing over all those long months, she was determined that Broer must be retired to a place where he would not be pushed to perform, where he could enjoy long trail rides and the love of someone who knew his mighty heart.

What she did was far from collecting the fat checks she was being offered. Amie *gave* Broer back to me. At that point, I could have never afforded him. But we are so right together, and to this day, he is the light of my life. He ensures that every day is Christmas for me, and we trust and love each other in a way that is unique and special to just us two. Shortly after Broer arrived, we rode in our first parade, completely decked out in medieval tack and regalia alongside my dear friend Kris Dawson, who also owned a Friesian. It was truly a dream come true for this girl with the turbulent past. The bond I felt with Kris, her horse, Kestrel, and my Broer on that day was beyond words.

A Lifelong Mission

Today my life is complete and wildly fulfilling in ways I never thought possible. My work at Moonlight Fund is profoundly meaningful, even if the need seems inexhaustible. There will always be new burn survivors, family members, and burn unit staff that require my help. While my marriage to Randy may have seemed odd to many, it worked for us. We were both committed to this mission of mine, and we both sacrificed on a regular basis.

I don't want or seek a life that fits into the norm. After years of thinking I could find acceptance if I could move up the next level in my career, or find that next level of social and financial stability, I know I am destined for a different path. This life I have is all mine. I love it, I am proud of it, and I would not change it for the world.

My views on death and sickness may seem disconcerting or odd to many people. I truly have no fear of death, as my lifestyle clearly shows. Maybe it's because I've already coded twice in this life, once as a child after my burn injuries and later as an adult in post-op. I know that spirituality is different for us all, but for me, it means peace, as it has ever since I was a child.

At some point, I learned that my mother had uterine cancer in her twenties. I lived with the fear all children know, that they may one day lose their beloved parent. Just when life finally seemed to be on track for my mother, she received the devastating diagnosis of breast cancer at the age of fifty. The world crashed in on both of us. The cancer was completely unconnected to her earlier bout in her twenties. From that time on, she was diagnosed with one cancer after another, every two to three years. Yet none of the cancers were systemic.

She was a rarity in the world of cancer, and to this day, her case is followed by some leading oncologists. When my mother finally crossed over at age seventy-two, I was alone with her. The things I saw and experienced were both incredible and beautiful. For me, that was the experience of the "spirit" part of me in full force. This incredible woman had never stopped golfing, bowling, or managing her accounting practice that she'd built up through hard work and sheer will. She was fully engaged right up until the end. For her, I was the daughter that was always the "go-to" for every issue, including my sister's substance abuse problems.

For many years, my own body has grown excessive tumors, and while none have been life threatening, they are very stressful and have demanded expensive and disruptive surgical intervention. I believe that all the years of surgeries and all my exposure to anesthesia—as well as narcotics—are significant. I wonder if they poison the body and contribute to these tumors.

Game Changer

I've experienced my share of health issues but on July 12, 2017, I had an experience that would forever change my life. My friend Bethany Coomes arrived to spend a couple days with me. As we sat on the back deck, she suggested we go for a ride. I saddled up Broer and Toranado and off we went. Toranado was a wild child, I loved riding him and as usual, he took off on me. I was too engrossed in conversation to have a good handle on him. I have no memory of that day; only what Bethany has told me.

She said that I attempted spinning him to the left, a tactic I often used with great success, but this time it didn't work. Broer joined in and both horses were at a dead run. Bethany was a novice rider and although I have no memories, I know exactly what I did. I threw the reins and pushed off. I had to stop both running horses to take care of Bethany. I landed, head first, on the hard asphalt. My maneuver worked; Broer, the horse Bethany was riding, stopped and came to me, allowing Bethany an easy dismount. To her horror, I laid motionless, all color gone from my body, my breathing shallow and the pool of blood surrounding my head was growing larger by the second. Bethany told me that she held it together, calling 911, attempting to describe where we were, which was the middle of nowhere. There were no homes or landmarks for her to describe, other than a distant water tower.

I know she must have been praying that I would not die there in front of her. It was 11:30 that night before I regained consciousness. Medical staff at University Hospital said my only response was, "Why? I have good insurance, why am I not at Methodist or Baptist?"

The nurse explained that I needed to be in a level one trauma center. She also went on to say that I was being moved to the neuro-surgical unit. I would be undergoing brain surgery to reduce the bleeding in my brain. I was grateful to look over and see Bethany standing there, although the pain on her face left no doubt that I was in serious condition. I spent three days in the hospital and I was never alone. Day and night, mothers and wives of burn survivors, my Moonlight Fund family took shifts and never left my side. Randy, who was working in Iowa at the time, jumped in his car and drove seventeen hours to be by my side and I remember thinking, "He really loves me."

My life today is a bit different. I suffer from seizures, maddening headaches, vertigo, balance issues and memory problems. Several lobes of my brain were damaged and my inner ear vestibular is permanently ruptured. It was a tough pill to swallow when the state medical board took away my driver's license. Freedom, Libertad, those two words that I have held so close to my heart were leaving me, bit by bit and I felt I was becoming a slave to doctors visits, medications and testing. Yet, as I always do, I found the damn humor in it all. In fact, vertigo is the best way to redecorate your home while never moving a thing and I should dye my hair blonde, for I am so dizzy these days. It's been an adjustment, however, and I am enjoying more time at home, caring for my land and animals. I'm not comfortable accepting rides from others; nonetheless, I have no choice and must adapt to this new life of mine. A role reversal of sorts has taken place and it is now my Moonlight Fund family, the wives and mothers of my burn survivors, who are caring for me. Although I found accepting their help difficult at first, I now find my time with them a blessing and I'm incredibly grateful for their support.

For many years I've said, "I'll go off the back of a horse, that's how I'll leave this world." A part of me felt robbed, this should have been it, I should have embraced Valhalla. As with everything, there is always a reason that we don't understand. I must embrace my "new norm" and I am determined to live my new life as fully as possible. My life has been filled with challenges and it is not for me to understand them; it is for me to break them.

Bethany struggled for quite some time, she carried such guilt and she blamed herself for having suggested we go riding. I explained to her on many occasions that all that happens in this life is meant to be, and the reasons for any and all suffering we endure will become evident to us in the future. We cannot grow in this life without tragedy, pain, and suffering. It took some time, but I think today she realizes it was all part of the master plan.

Photo shoot for an equine magazine with Merlin and Broer

My "wild child" Lexell

Merlin and my German Shepherd, Moby

Hillary, age 14

Photo shoot in the rain with my two boys, Toranado and Broer

My first two imported Friesians, Merlin and Broer

The birth of Sansei

My brother Mark, my father, and my cousin, David, with my mother's horse, Stormy

The last photo of Sansei, taken the evening before I sold her

Randy and me in Africa

Blue wildebeest shot during my trip to Namibia

Will never forget the thrill of petting this cheetah in Africa

Randy and me, September 2009

My last kill — an elusive warthog

Shot this springbok at 185 yards

Randy with one of his finest trophies, a monster kudu

Randy and me among the giraffes

Omatako Hunting Trails, Namibia, Africa — our honeymoon

CHAPTER NINE

As I Am

Treasure........

Fill your pockets with the treasure of this world...

Protect your mind and all those memories you treasure
Embrace the treasure you hold in your heart...

But, in the end, the treasures we store up in this life, will mean nothing
Your pockets will be empty, your mind void and your heart still...

All you have here...will remain here...

For, in the new life, you will have so much more
Your regrets, vengeance and faith will no longer serve you
You are free...A new life awaits you...in the midst of a peaceful mountain...

Travel with those who have gone before, learn and listen
For in the end...Kindness is all that matters....

C Returns with a Vengeance

Not long before my mother crossed over, I got word that my beloved baby sister, Audra, then just thirty-seven years old, had cancer as well. It was not just any cancer but neuroendocrine cancer, which was rare, deadly, and extremely difficult to treat. She had surgery to remove the tumor and the doctors predicted a three-year survival period for her. Sixteen months later, the tumor came back. I struggled with the thought that my beloved baby, my Audra, would leave me.

My daughter, Hillary, had done some extensive research and developed an organic, macrobiotic diet for Audra, sharing with her information on supplements, etc. I was on the phone with Audra one day and we were walking through this information as I was preparing a "care package" to send to her. She interrupted me and asked, "Sissy, can I come there to be with you?"

I immediately booked a flight for her and her five-year-old daughter. When they arrived at the airport, I was shocked. My five-foot ten-inch sister weighed little more than eighty pounds. The next day, I took her to the hospital and asked that she get a feeding tube and IV fluids. Three days into her stay, I received a call that she was being discharged and she had been labeled non-compliant. This was a result of her plan to return to my home and get well without the help of an oncologist. She had shared her plans with the medical staff and was immediately reported to higher-ups. I know my way around a hospital, and I was completely unafraid to fight with the powers-that-be regarding our holistic approach to her treatment. She needed that feeding tube kept in place for us to adequately nourish her. In the end, she and her daughter lived with us for two months. Hillary was the one who truly knew how to administer the diet. When Audra returned home and had a PET scan, the tumor was gone. Her doctors were at a loss how to explain how such a large, life-threatening tumor could simply vanish. Heartbreakingly, it returned again eighteen months later, this time on her larynx.

We spoke often about the fact that she would no longer have the ability to talk. I delicately attempted to persuade her to make some videos for her children and grandchildren. Read them a book, tell them how much you love them, just anything, but please, leave your voice for us to cherish as we know we will never hear it again. She had surgery to remove the tumor, and I never heard my baby sister's voice again. This heartbreak is tough to describe and even tougher to live.

The next summer, she and her daughter Trynattee enjoyed an extended visit at my ranch. As you can imagine, I had to learn how to communicate with her via written word and I felt the heartache of not hearing her tender and loving voice. I was amazed at how she and her young daughter had adapted, developing a series of verbal clucks, hand gestures, and sign language to communicate. My baby sister had grown into a woman of strength and determination and I found myself loving her even more.

Audra's cancer returned with a vengeance in June of 2017. She was covered head to foot with metastatic neuroendocrine carcinoma tumors. Her doctors prepared her for the pain and suffering to come, yet she was grateful for the extra years she spent with her children. By this time she had an electrolarynx, a medical device used to produce sound for those who have lost their voice box. This device allowed us to talk, and although it may not have been "her" voice, the sweet, loving and melodic cadence of her voice was the same. I was allowed to enjoy those last precious conversations with my baby sister. She told me that it was OK, that she was ready for the pain and equally ready to see mom and she began and ended each conversation in the same way, "I love you, Sissy."

Audra left us on October 14, 2017. While that shock was enough for anyone to absorb, two weeks later life grew even more grave. My husband, my beloved Randy, was diagnosed with glioblastoma, brain cancer. My entire world was about to shatter.

Randy called me on a Tuesday morning with the news and my immediate response was, "Come home and I'll take care of you." He had a different plan, having already begun a process with a doctor in Iowa. Randy was determined to have the tumor removed, and remain in Iowa to continue his work building a Microsoft data center. I arranged for animal care at home and cleared my calendar. Taboo and I arrived in Iowa on Thanksgiving Day. The Randy I once knew, the workaholic, athletic man with the generous heart, was failing, and it was obvious. I knew I was going to lose him, the world was also about to lose him. His prognosis was that he had three to four months to live without radiation and chemo, or about twelve months with treatment.

I knew I had to engage Randy in some very clear conversations regarding just how his life would end. We discussed medications, treatments, living arrangements and care. I was firm and loving, yet, I knew that things would soon become difficult and that Randy's wishes needed to be voiced now, while he could still do so, and I honored every one of them.

Randy and I are not believers in chemo or radiation treatments. We often talked about how we would leave this world and that neither of us would subject ourselves to such poison. Yet, the intense pressure on his brain was more than he could bear, and he went ahead with the surgery. He was desperate for some relief and they were successful in removing a tennis ball sized portion of the tumor.

With the large mass removed, he was back to the old Randy, barking orders at me, doing the same by phone with coworkers. His greatest desire was to come home, be with me, the animals, the sunsets, and the land that we both loved. I arranged a Medjet flight for him and we arrived home on December 6, 2017. That evening it began to snow, something quite rare in this part of Texas. It was as if God was bringing me the snow of my youth combined with the Texas I loved. With Randy by my side, I knew I was truly home.

Randy's dear friend, Mark Leight, arrived a few days later. Randy thought so highly of Mark, not just as a friend, but as a leader and co-worker in the commercial building world. Randy was never a man of many words, but I always knew that Mark was more like a brother to him. We enjoyed the next six days together, caring for Randy and reminiscing. Each of us shared stories of our time with this incredible man. We found laughter daily in some of Randy's care and I believe Randy enjoyed that also. After Mark left, I spent the next week not only caring for Randy, but remaining with him even as he slept; each moment was a precious gift. I loved listening to his breathing and taking in the shape of his face. He was not emaciated from treatments, he was simply weak due to his illness. The man I looked upon remained the same, strong man I had fallen in love with all those years ago.

As you might imagine, I had not decorated for the holidays, nor did I have many gifts pulled together for the children. My friend Leigh Ann Kenney, the wife of a burn survivor, came by and wrapped the few gifts I had. My treasured friend, Catrina Kendrick, sent over a Christmas tree, complete with lights and ornaments.

Randy was never a Christmas kind of guy. Yet each year he went the extra mile, cooking wonderful dishes for me and the children. The morning of December 23, my phone rang. I heard the always upbeat and loving voice of Bethany, the mother of a burn survivor, wife of one of our former burn unit nurses, and now one of my dearest friends. I shared with her that Randy was close.

Over the years, I've developed the "curse" or "gift" of predicting death, usually to the day. On this day, I wished I didn't have it. She asked if I was alone, which of course I was other than the occasional visit of the hospice nurse. Bethany said she was coming over. Not long into our visit we stepped out onto the porch. There we saw a very large bird approach, out of a sunset that seemed so conflicted this evening. Our sunsets usually streak the sky with an abundance of colors. But on this night, the sunset contained very little color, occupying only the left portion of the sky. The shape was more tornadic than expansive, with dark, swirling colors.

As quickly as the bird approached, it changed directions and headed back into the sunset. Bethany and I looked at each other with a strange sense of knowing. We quickly went to Randy's side and it was clear he was close to crossing over. I grabbed my stethoscope and jumped into the bed with him, searching his chest frantically for any sound. I heard just one last, faint beat of his heart. Our dog, Taboo, was next to me. As Randy's life left his body, Taboo began vigorously licking his face, as if he had a new pup and it was both beautiful and heartbreaking.

As shock turned to reality, I felt the need to be as close to Randy as possible. I stretched my body over top of him and laid there for nearly two hours. I felt his body grow cold under me and it wasn't morbid, it was beautiful. Our spirits were together then, as they always had been and will remain so. At one point, I looked over to Bethany and asked, "Is he really gone?" She answered in the kindest of voice. "Yes, Celia, he is." And with that, I left him.

When staff arrived to remove Randy's body, there was a huge part of me that wanted to scream out, "No, you can't take him!" Bethany and the hospice nurse sensed my mood and remained calm and comforting by my side. Randy crossed over at 6:20 on December 23, 2017.

During those last days, Randy and I reminisced about our life together and he never stopped telling me how much he loved me and I never stopped kissing him. The thought of continuing in this life without him rips at my soul. Yet I know full well he will always look after me and the Moonlight Fund.

We had 3,062 days together, and I know those were the best days of my life. He had few words in those last days, other than Celia, love and water. Randy did share one thing with me a few weeks before he passed: "I've done nothing in this life good other than the Moonlight Fund." This caught me off guard and confused me. I reminded him of his nephew, sister, friends and the multitude of people he mentored through his work.

He responded with something that will always stay with me, saying, "That was all expected." I've given those words much consideration. Randy was a deeply thoughtful and caring person and I realized what he was saying. Yes, we do have things in this life that are expected of us. And we have things that we choose to do to better the lives of others. I now fully realize that Randy was as invested in the efforts of Moonlight Fund as I was. It was not just about me; it was about us.

Randy's words and his spirit give me the strength I need to pick up the pieces of a shattered life and rebuild my future. I have an odd sense of peace that alternates with anguish because I believe the world after this one is full of experiences and knowledge. Yet I am not immune to the pain I feel in my heart. I believe that crossing over offers us a time to grow, explore, and understand. The pain I may feel here when I lose a loved one is nothing compared to the ultimate adventure they'll experience on the other side. Perhaps this belief is part of why I ride wild horses, skydive, seek out the highest zip lines, and hunt dangerous game. I do live on the edge with little fear of death. For isn't death just another part of life?

I arranged a service for Randy and people from across the country, many of whom had worked with him, arrived to share in this celebration of his life. I was deeply touched by their stories and there was a consistent message in all of them: Randy was greatly admired, respected and loved by all. There was also another message they brought, and that was how much Randy adored me and was so proud of the work I did with Moonlight Fund.

They shared how Randy kept my photo as his screen saver, how he spoke constantly of me and the fact that he was quick to share the Moonlight Fund website with them. This man of few words had found many words to describe to others the love he had for me, and the work I do.

I needed to hear all of that. In the few years prior to Randy's passing, as with any relationship, things had been difficult between us. Randy and I had worked our way through three major issues with his health. This had taken its toll, as well as living apart, due to his work. It was not an easy life. I spent several days with these people and perhaps the most heart-wrenching moment was when his coworkers from Iowa arrived with a duffle bag. My trembling fingers found the zipper. As I opened the bag, I could feel Randy with me, and I began to smell his sweet, musky scent.

The bag contained assorted items, including Randy's hard hat, vests and jacket, each bearing his name. I pulled the items out slowly and listened to the stories his coworkers shared. It was an emotional time for us all, reading his name on all those possessions and softly speaking it aloud as I ran my hands over the letters embroidered on his jacket. I could do nothing but cry and repeat his name again and again.

It didn't take long for me to decide that my husband's ashes needed to be spread at Omatako, in Namibia, where we had spent our honeymoon. I invited my friend Leigh Ann to accompany me. As I booked the trip and made plans, it occurred to me that if I was taking Randy, why not take Audra also. So, as it goes, they will both lie there, in what I consider "heaven," under the deep blue sky, and the star-filled nights, surrounded by the wild and wonderful creatures of that land. I will join them there someday, when my time comes, and I will know the peace and love of them all over again.

As I painfully adjusted to life without Randy, I realized March of 2018 was fast approaching. I knew I would be needed at the DAR event to accept the Daughters of the American Revolution Distinguished Citizen Medal. As the day approached, I nearly panicked. I had not spoken publicly since my accident and Randy had made plans to be my side for this honor. I felt lost as I prepared, how could I speak without him and the immense honor of this award was overwhelming. Several of the wounded military members assisted by Moonlight Fund were with me. Their friendship and love held me together.

At one point, I was asked to leave them and sit at the head table. I am usually a very well-put-together person. Public speaking, social events, fundraising were all second nature to me, but, since the accident and losing both my baby sister and my husband, I was not the woman I once was. Bethany, who was one of the guests immediately sensed my apprehension and fear and with her kind eyes, she nudged me forward. As dinner was served I made polite talk with DAR State Chair, Kathy Hanlon, and with my dog Taboo by my side, I felt I was making it through. Then the time came when Madame State Regent, Judy Callaway Ostler, stood up to make my introduction and Kathy Hanlon carried on with my bio and achievements.

There were more than a thousand people in the audience, and as Kathy began to speak a large screen began to roll photos of my life that the DAR had pulled during their vetting process. The first photo was of Randy and me. I had to look away, the pain I felt was palpable and my eyes landed on the table filled with the military burn survivors and their spouses in attendance and a calm came over me that is beyond what I'd ever felt before. When my time came, I stood, accepted the medal and approached the mic. I tossed the notes I had transcribed to the side and in that moment I "owned it." I spoke from my heart and into the hearts of those seated and I know Randy was right by my side.

———•◆•———

I've lived a big life. I've done far more than many people will ever have the chance to do, and today I fully embrace the totality of my experience and recognize the blessings in my life. Even though my younger years were dark, I've been extremely blessed in my adult life with abundant happiness and incredible experiences. All those dreams I dreamed on my front porch while escaping my home life, well, many came true.

I was one of the lucky ones, I met and married the love of my life and realized what true love is. I also enjoy the love and security found in family and friends. At the end of the day, there is both beauty and balance in my life. I share my story in the humble hope that others who dream big and who struggle with adversity and setbacks will be inspired to cherish and nourish those dreams and to keep hope alive even in dark times. I also hope that you found a good laugh while observing this life of mine, because I've been laughing for most of the process and I'll keep right on finding amusement in both the tragedy and in the fun.

Out of my personal traumas came a mission much bigger than I can ever be by myself. I was somehow given the gift to understand that in all pain there's a new level of growth available to us and we must step back from that pain and freely accept the lessons, embracing them in totality and humbling ourselves before God and his mighty plan. I pray daily that the mighty strength I've been forced to forge in this life will carry me on into the next.

I've found it much easier to find the humor in my experiences than to dwell on the negative. I've lived much of my life by my friend's words, "laugh you live, cry you die." My path to a life of meaning may not have been straight or easy, but I am fortunate to have found my personal stepping stones laid out before me like a masterpiece. There is not one stone, not one memory or one experience that I would have changed. I am grateful for the good and the bad, for I am the sum of all my experiences. For many years, I avoided becoming close to those I assist. Yet they have become so dear to me and occupy a place in my heart and my life that can be shared with no other. I'm extremely blessed to walk that path among my family. No, not my blood family, but my burn family. In them I have found the love and acceptance that always eluded me. My time spent with them, even during times of my own turmoil, brings me back to center and reminds me of just how powerful survival and love can be. I will be forever grateful to them, for they have provided me a life of servitude and meaning. For in the end kindness is all that matters, and it is through our selfless acts and kind ways that each of us will remain... *Remarkably Intact.*

Audra and my son, Justin, during her last visit to Texas

My sister, Audra

Audra with her daughter, Trynattee

Broer and me, Medieval Ready, 2017

Hillary, age 20

Surrounded by the mothers, daughters, and wives of burn survivors, "my tribe," 2018

Bethany and me, remaining strong after weathering many a storm in 2017

My Broer — truly the horse of a lifetime

Hillary, cover shot for her spread in
Current Magazine

*My acceptance speech at the DAR
awards ceremony, March 2018*

*Accepting the Daughters of the American Revolution award
from Kathy Hanlon and Madame Regent, Judy Calloway Ostler*

*Dr. Susan Garrison, Blaine Scott, me and MyTaboo, Madame
Regent, Judy Callaway Ostler, Ed Matayka and Shilo Harris*

My children, Jarred, Hillary, and Justin, and me

Hillary and me, 2018

Randy and me in Mexico City, 2014

Randy and me shortly after arriving in Africa

Randy and me at home in Texas

Us, forever and after

At the end of the day, each of us has the choice of how to live it

I choose heaven

Heroes

" THE THIRD TIMES A CHARM "
DOESN'T APPLY
TO A MAN WHO REFUSES
TO BREAK.
—ALEX

Help the Moonlight Fund provide the financial and emotional
support burn survivors **so desperately need by going to**
WWW.MOONLIGHTFUND.ORG

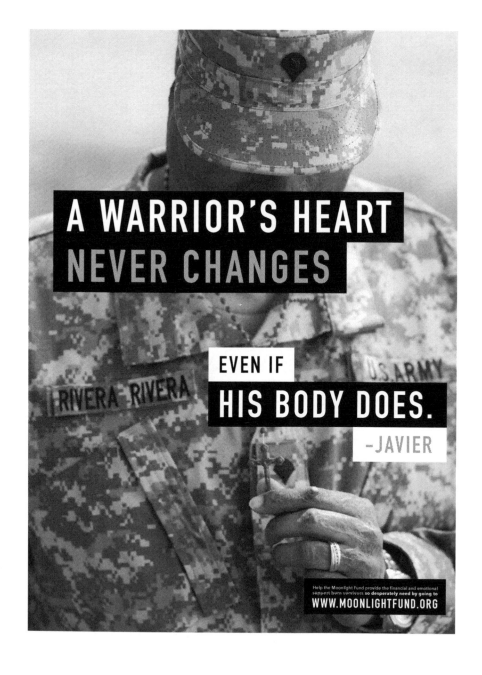

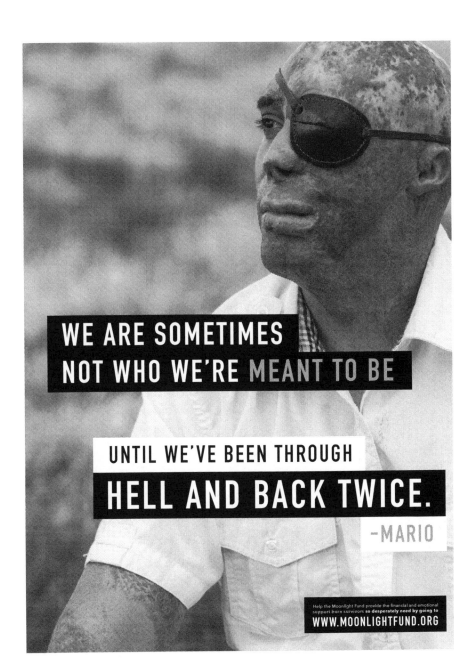

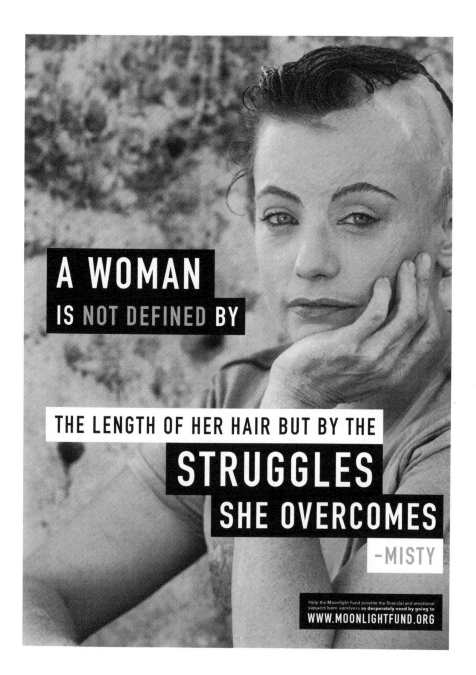

Acknowledgments

I'd like to acknowledge the thousands of burn survivors and their family members whom I've worked with for more than 20 years. Your strength has made me a stronger person and helped me to rise to new heights in my quest to help others. I must also acknowledge Deborah Ortiz Da La Pena. Your gentle spirit and encouragement offered to me several years ago set me on the path to write this book, something I had always said "no" to in the past. I will be forever grateful to you for allowing me to open my soul, share my story, and enjoy healing on an entirely new level. Thank you.

Author

Celia Belt is the founder of the award-winning, Moonlight Fund Inc., a 501(c)(3) non profit organization that provides financial and emotional assistance to burn survivors and their families. A burn survivor herself, Celia recognized the need for survivor care. Along with Henry Coffeen III, she started the Texas-based charity in 1998. Since then, the organization has helped nearly 10,000 burn survivors across the United States.

Celia oversees grant writing, program development, event planning and fundraising for the Moonlight Fund. She provides support to burn survivors and their families by visiting them at the hospital and hosting support groups. She also organizes and executes award-winning healing retreats for burn survivors and their families.

Before starting Moonlight Fund, Celia had a successful career in commercial and residential real estate. She also spent seven years as a national sales manager for food manufacturer VanHolten's, where she was instrumental in product development and marketing.

In 2012, Celia was invited to speak at the Pentagon on behalf of Moonlight Fund when the charity was named the top non profit in the country and given the Fisher House/Newman's Own Award for improving the quality of life of military members and their families. Celia continues to speak on topics that include the needs of burn survivors, non profit management, overcoming childhood trauma, and empowerment for women.

Additionally, Celia has been awarded the *San Antonio Business Journal*'s Women in Leadership Award. She was chosen as a mentor three years running for the *Business Journal*'s Mentoring Monday event. Most recently, Celia was presented with the Distinguished Citizen Medal by the Daughters of the American Revolution.

Originally from Rockford, Illinois, and now a Bandera, Texas resident, Celia has published various articles in prominent publications including *San Antonio Medical Magazine* and *Game Trails*. When Celia is not caring for burn survivors, serving on committees, or writing grants, she enjoys spending time with her adult children and her grandson. She has been an equestrian for many years and enjoys riding on her ranch.

Visit **www.remarkablyintact.com** to view additional photos. Learn more about Celia at **www.celiabelt.com**.

———◆·◆·◆———

Alison Raffalovich has 30 years of ghost writing and communications experience in the corporate and non profit arenas. She received her MBA from the University of Texas at Austin and a BA in Business from Michigan State University, both degrees in marketing. She has written opinion pieces, guest editorials, speeches and lengthy articles for senior executives and not-for-profit leaders in a range of functions, which have been published in trade and business publications across North America and Europe.

About Moonlight Fund

Moonlight Fund was founded in 1998 by Celia Belt, Henry Coffeen lll, executives at Ernst & Young, and staff at Brooke Army Medical Center. Burn Unit. Emotional, financial and in-kind support are made available to burn survivors and their family members, and to those who have lost a loved one to a burn injury. Founding principles of low overhead/high giving and 24/7 care remain in place to this day. The fund was chosen as the top non profit in the U.S. in 2012 and awarded the Fisher House/Newman's Own Foundation Award for Excellence. The organization has received numerous other awards over the years. Visit www.moonlightfund.org to learn more.

Made in the
USA
Columbia, SC